Reflective Supervision in Education

T0385244

of related interest

Practical Supervision
How to Become a Supervisor for the Helping Professions
Jim Holloway, Anthea Millar and Penny Henderson
Foreword by Brigid Proctor and Francesca Inskipp
ISBN 978 1 84905 442 3
eISBN 978 0 85700 918 0

Best Practice in Professional Supervision
A Guide for the Helping Professions
Allyson Davys and Liz Beddoe
ISBN 978 1 84310 995 2
eISBN 978 0 85700 384 3

Passionate Supervision
Robin Shohet
ISBN 978 1 84310 556 5
eISBN 978 1 84642 749 7

Supporting Staff Mental Health in Your School
Amy Sayer
Foreword by Pooky Knightsmith
ISBN 978 1 78775 463 8
eISBN 978 1 78775 464 5

The Mentally Healthy Schools Workbook
Practical Tips, Ideas, Action Plans and Worksheets for Making Meaningful Change
Pooky Knightsmith
Foreword by Norman Lamb
ISBN 978 1 78775 148 4
eISBN 978 1 78775 149 1

The Mental Health and Wellbeing Handbook for Schools
Transforming Mental Health Support on a Budget
Clare Erasmus
Foreword by Chris Edwards
ISBN 978 1 78592 481 1
eISBN 978 1 78450 869 2

REFLECTIVE SUPERVISION in EDUCATION

*Using Supervision to Support
Pupil and Staff Wellbeing*

Hollie Edwards

Foreword by Pooky Knightsmith

Jessica Kingsley Publishers
London and Philadelphia

First published in Great Britain in 2023 by Jessica Kingsley Publishers
An imprint of John Murray Press

1

A CIP catalogue record for this title is available from the
British Library and the Library of Congress

ISBN 978 1 83997 410 6
eISBN 978 1 83997 411 3

Printed and bound by CPI Group (UK) Ltd, Croydon, CR0 4YY

Jessica Kingsley Publishers' policy is to use papers that are natural,
renewable and recyclable products and made from wood grown in
sustainable forests. The logging and manufacturing processes are expected
to conform to the environmental regulations of the country of origin.

Jessica Kingsley Publishers
Carmelite House
50 Victoria Embankment
London EC4Y 0DZ

www.jkp.com

John Murray Press
Part of Hodder & Stoughton Limited
An Hachette UK Company

This book is for Charlie, Daisy, George, Sienna and Oliver. I wouldn't have finished it without your support, patience and the endless cups of tea you made me. Your belief in me never faltered, even when mine did. Thank you for being my greatest supporters.

Contents

Foreword

My work as a keynote speaker and mental health educator takes me all over the UK and beyond, where I get the joy and privilege of working with different schools and settings every week. I've developed a bit of a spidey sense for what a mentally healthy school feels like, and that spidey sense told me I was in a safe, happy place indeed on the sunny day that Hollie showed me around her school.

It just felt good. Children, and adults, were laughing, kindness abounded and I ran into little examples of curiosity, pride and healthy challenge wherever I went. There was a quiet, calm buzz about the place, and as an anxious, autistic adult who was a stranger to the school, I quickly felt a sense of belonging, connection, joy and calm. The more digging I did, the more I was convinced of my first impressions, that this was a very mentally healthy school where students, staff and the wider community were thriving. But why?

Of course, the answer to that question was manifold, and a huge amount of work has happened, and continues, to ensure an inclusive, mentally healthy school. But one of the answers to that question is, undoubtedly, staff supervision. Supervision is one of those things that I recommend all the time; I've been banging on about it for years since experiencing its transformational qualities when I got hoodwinked into leading some reflective practice groups early on in my career. A wise colleague was ahead of the curve on this and came from a background where supervision was the norm. Her response was to set up a series of training sessions on topics that staff were desperate for, such as self-harm, eating disorders, anxiety and depression, back in a time when there was far less understanding of such things. The quid pro quo, for both the attendees and for me as the trainer, was that in addition to the regular training sessions, there would be regular space for reflective practice. I got taught to lead these sessions that were designed to enable colleagues to experience the power of group supervision, and give them the tools they needed to take the approach back to their own settings and set up their own groups.

I was cynical, especially as, while an experienced trainer, this was pretty new to me. I felt like the time would have been better spent on more training and sharing practical ideas.

I was wrong.

We had six sessions together. They were transformative, for me as well as for my charges. We bonded, we grew in confidence, we learned how to move forwards with problems that might not have (or need) solutions; each person realized they were not alone and several people shed burdens they'd carried alone since childhood. Our sessions gave them the confidence, strength and impetus to seek help for past trauma that was having a very real impact in their present. We started those sessions as a group of individuals unsure as to why we were there. We left as a team who had bonded and grown in ways that felt inexplicable given the simplicity of the sessions.

This simple magic is something I think every educator should be allowed to experience and from which every member of school staff would benefit, especially in the current climate where staff wellbeing is at an all-time low and student mental health issues are at an all-time high.

So when Hollie was proudly showing me around her school and she mentioned that she believed that staff supervision had played a part in the culture they'd achieved, I jumped into Spanish Inquisition mode. Why did they start? Who was doing it? How did they get it going? Did staff have buy-in? Was it having an impact? How did they find time? And on and on and on.

Hollie answered all my questions. My excitement was building the whole time because while I think that staff supervision is a good idea and a transformative process, I have rarely encountered down-to-earth examples of good practice that felt proven and repeatable by any school prepared to invest the time and energy to try and get it right. While it's increasingly common for one or two leaders to receive external supervision (hurrah!), internal, staff-wide supervision is rare, and the barriers can feel insurmountable to many, the biggest barrier being understanding the practicalities of the 'what' and the 'how'.

So when Hollie shyly told me that she was writing a book on the topic based on her experiences developing and delivering a model of supervision in her school, I was *ecstatic*, and when she asked me to write the Foreword, I did a little happy skip. This is the book that every school needs to make a difference to the wellbeing of their students, staff and wider community. Buying the book is only the first step, of course – it's what you do with it that matters – but I think you'll find that Hollie has made this all feel very doable. She's walked you through what she did and how you can make it work in your setting too. If there are leaders or governors you need to convince (or if you're still on the fence yourself), then Chapters 1–4 will give you all the evidence and context you need.

If you are up for the idea but are not sure what would work best in your setting, or who might be able to lead the process (perhaps you're wondering if it could be you...it could!), take a romp through Chapters 5 and 6. Once you're ready to get down to the nitty-gritty and actually do this thing, the second half of the book, from Chapter 6 onwards, tells you everything you need to know and includes incredibly helpful things, like a sample policy, questions for use in your settings, Hollie's three C's for the supervisory environment (confidentiality, comfort and consistency) and a wide range of questions and prompts that can be used within sessions that have worked well for Hollie and others in the past.

The final two chapters focus on evaluation and reflection so you can measure the impact of these processes in your setting. Don't skip this part of the process as it is possibly the most affirming exercise you'll carry out in your professional career. I hope that in a few months' time, you'll have gone from holding this book in your hands for the first time filled with hope, ideas and probably a little trepidation to having helped to implement a practice that has been transformative for you and for your colleagues.

This book matters. Thank you for reading it, and for the steps you'll take to make a difference in your school. I really hope Hollie's guidance enables you to go out and do. I hope you'll be inspired to share what you learn with colleagues in your network. Perhaps you'll gift a copy of this 'why and how to' book to someone in another school, telling them, as I'm telling you, that it has everything they need to get started and that they can make this work, if they want to.

Please be brave and try these ideas, and if you need any cheerleading along the way, or if you're struggling with a particular hurdle or you'd like to share your pride in the difference you're making, Hollie and I would love to hear from you. We're both regular tweeters – @Pookyh and @Holliee84 – and we'd both love to hear about your journey with supervision.

Good luck and thank you for all that you're doing.

Pooky
Dr Pooky Knightsmith, keynote speaker,
author and mental health educator
www.pookyknightsmith.com

Acknowledgements

I would like to thank Lisa Lea Weston, the founder of Talking Heads,[1] for being so eager to write about external supervision for senior leaders. Her extensive experience and knowledge on the subject is evident in her writing, but what really shines through is her passion for supervision in education. The headteachers and senior leaders she supervises are incredibly fortunate and, in turn, so are the staff and pupils at their schools.

I want to thank the headteacher of Herne Bay Junior School, Melody Kingman, an inspirational leader, colleague and friend. Without your vision, passion and absolute determination to provide staff and children with the best possible learning environment, this book would not have happened. Thank you for your support and belief in what I, and the whole school, can achieve when we work together.

I also want to thank my colleagues for being so open and willing to engage with supervision. Your hard work and dedication to the children inspires me every day.

Thank you to my tutor and supervisor, Netta Bowden. I can only hope to be as knowledgeable as you one day.

Finally, I want to thank my Year 6 teacher, Mr Lucas, for his kindness and humour. You will never know how much it meant to me.

---

1 https://talkingheadssupervision.co.uk

Preface

I have worked in education for a little over seven years, in a large junior school. I qualified as a counsellor in 2013 after deciding at primary school that I wanted to work in psychology in one way or another. From my own childhood experiences, I also knew I wanted to work with children, so when I began looking for a job as a counsellor, I approached my local school. Unfortunately, like many schools, they did not have the budget for a school counsellor but they were looking for a family liaison officer. I enjoyed the role of supporting children, and their families, and I was able to offer counselling as part of my role too. After a few years, as more children struggled with their mental health and general wellbeing, it became apparent that my role needed to change. I joined the senior leadership team and took on the (newly developed) role of Director of Mental Health and Wellbeing. As a team, we decided that we wanted (and needed!) to focus on a whole-school approach to mental health and wellbeing, so the school set out to achieve the Carnegie Centre of Excellence for Mental Health in Schools Award.[2] The process highlighted what we already knew – that in order for children to achieve their full potential, they need to feel safe and secure, with a sense of belonging.

---

2   www.leedsbeckett.ac.uk/research/carnegie-centre-of-excellence-for-mental-health-in-schools

I believe my own, mixed experiences of school have led me down the path I am on now. When I was eight, my parents separated and there were some difficult times in the years that followed. The support I did (or did not, in some cases) receive made a huge difference to not only my life at the time, but it has continued to shape how I conduct myself personally and professionally as an adult. Sadly, my teacher (at the time of my parents' separation) did not understand my situation or empathize with me, and I spent most of the year in her class struggling. At school, my emotional needs were unmet so I couldn't engage with schoolwork. I still recall her telling my parents that I would not achieve well academically, and as she could not see my potential, neither did I. She did not see me; I was invisible. Thankfully, my experience the following year was very different. My teacher did notice me, my strengths (art, in this case), and praised every drawing I did. He framed the pictures I gave him and hung them in his house (or so he told me!). He encouraged me to show them to the rest of the class. He got to know me and my family. He recognized my potential and believed in me; I thrived in his class. Surprisingly (or not so surprisingly, as I now know!), I began excelling in other subjects too, and finished the year above expected for my age. Most importantly, though, I was engaged at school again and felt happy.

My secondary school experience was also up and down, although I do remember caring and compassionate members of staff taking the time to get to know me. The positive relationships I had with some teachers have stuck with me, and I am so grateful for the kindness I was shown. My own experiences act as a constant reminder of how pivotal staff are in the lives of children and young people – not only in their academic outcomes but also in shaping how they view themselves throughout their lives. They become the internal voices that have the potential to lift you up or pull you down. The responsibility is huge, but teachers are only human too. As a counsellor, I am expected to attend supervision each month. I often leave the sessions feeling emotionally lighter, with renewed clarity and a greater sense of awareness. I have no doubt that I am a better practitioner because of supervision. School staff are responsible for carrying a significant emotional load, one that is taking its toll. It saddens and frustrates me that there is currently no framework in education that provides emotional support to staff.

So why supervision? This question is explored in detail in Chapters 1–4, but for now, reflective supervision provides a space for staff to share professional challenges and work through them in a safe and supportive environment. It is also a space for professional development, a place where staff can gain a greater understanding of their pupils' needs, share advice and offer guidance to colleagues. I truly believe that if my primary teacher had received supervision, my experience that year would have been very different. Coincidently, I now work at my old primary school, and as reflective supervision is now part of the school culture, no child will feel invisible again.

My hope is that this book will help schools (and those that are part of decision making in education) to see the importance of supervision. Hopefully one day it will be part of a wider, systemic shift in education, but for now, every school that has chosen to buy this book has the power to make a change. A whole-school approach to mental health and wellbeing should be at the heart of every school. If you are wondering where or how to begin your journey, reflective supervision is a good place to start.

CHAPTER 1

What is 'Supervision'?

The term 'supervision' is often misunderstood in education, in part due to the meaning of the word itself, and partly due to the fact it is not widely practised in schools. It may evoke thoughts of line management, targets and appraisals. To understand its meaning, it is helpful to break the word into two – super + vision – the ability to see things more clearly. Supervision provides an opportunity for reflection, and through this, the practitioner gains a greater understanding of themselves and the work they do. This awareness is key to continued professional growth and development. While in other professions, such as social work and counselling, supervision is common practice, data from the *Teacher Wellbeing Index 2020* (Education Support 2020) shows that only 8 per cent of school staff have access to supervision, or a safe space to discuss issues. In the 2021 report, the data found that while 10 per cent of school leaders receive supervision, only 5 per cent of teachers and support staff do.

The impact of this lack of support in education is detrimental not only to staff but also to the children and young people they are teaching. Providing regular supervision to staff ensures that they remain healthy and well in their job role so they can spend more time working at their best than would otherwise be possible. As Hawkins and Shohet state, 'lack of supervision can contribute to feelings of staleness, rigidity and defensiveness which can very easily occur in professions that require us to give so much of ourselves' (2012, p.6). In providing supervision to education staff, they are supported to work through the stress and vicarious trauma they may experience in their job role, without judgement or blame, and this alone can offer a huge sense of relief. Education staff recognize they need a supportive space for this but, currently, schools do not have the structures in place that other professions do, such as in health and social care. As explored further in Chapter 2, this lack of structure is greatly impacting the mental health and general wellbeing of school staff.

Supervision should not be confused with therapy, although it is therapeutic due to its supportive and reflective nature. Inevitably, personal issues may arise in supervision, and it is important for them to be acknowledged, but the focus should remain on how those issues affect the individual's work and working relationships: 'Good supervision inevitably focuses some of its attention on the dynamics of the supervisees, but this must always arise out of work-related issues and be done in the service of understanding and being able to manage the work better' (Hawkins and Shohet 2012, p.53).

In their groundbreaking book *Supervision in the Helping Professions*, Hawkins and Shohet point out that supervision thrives in a learning environment, that 'An organization that is learning and developing right from the top down to the bottom is far more likely to be meeting the needs of the clients, because it is also meeting the needs of staff' (2012, p.235). Of course, in schools we are aiming to meet the needs of pupils, not 'clients', but the fundamental philosophy is still the same – teachers are best able to facilitate learning if they are supported to constantly learn and develop themselves. Supervision provides a space for this continued professional development. Jane Reed wrote about this in her chapter 'Freeing the Passion to Learn' in *Passionate Supervision*:

The literature that has been written about professional learning for teachers in the last 30 years suggests that teachers flourish when they can find a space to reflect on their practice, learn with and from each other and have enough opportunity to talk about what they are doing and what concerns them... This can then enable them to be as available as they possibly can for their pupils and in that relationship free up the passion to learn that is the joint endeavour of the learning and teaching relationship. (Reed 2008, pp.178–179)

There are numerous elements to supervision (and the needs of each supervisee are different), but, put simply, supervision offers a professional, reflective space that ensures good, ethical practice in an educational and supportive relationship. To ensure this is achieved in supervision, it is important to understand its functions.

The functions of supervision

There are many theoretical approaches and models to supervision, each with their own framework and functions. Some models offer a clear structure to supervision and others are based on a set of principles that can help guide your approach to it. While it is useful to have an understanding of the development and theory of supervision, for the purpose of this book, we will only touch on one model that fits well with reflective supervision, the 'model of clinical supervision'.

This model originates from counselling supervision. Inskipp and Proctor (1993) identify the three main tasks of supervision as *normative*, *formative* and *restorative*. Using these functions, Proctor later introduced the supervision alliance model in *Fundamental Themes in Clinical Supervision* (2001). The model 'assumes that practitioners are usually keen to work well, and to be self-monitoring, if they are brought to professional maturity in a learning environment which sufficiently values, supports and challenges them' (Proctor 2010, p.24). With a safe and trusting environment, reflective practice is a skill that can be learned. The ability to reflect honestly on practice and experience is a vital skill for professional learning and development.

As already touched on, the three main tasks of supervision (normative, formative and restorative) are a well-known feature of the supervision alliance model, and they provide a useful framework for reflective supervision in schools (see Figure 1.1).[1]

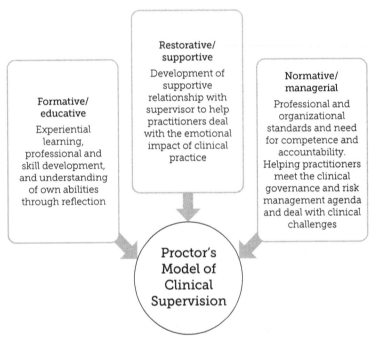

Figure 1.1: Proctor's model of clinical supervision

There are a number of key components that, when put together, ensure the functions of supervision are achieved:

- It takes place within a trusting relationship

1   www.researchgate.net/figure/Proctors-model-of-clinical-supervision-Proctor-2008_fig1_347233232

- It is confidential

- It is ongoing and regular

- It is boundaried

- It is a safe, non-judgemental space to express and explore emotions

- It offers a space for reflection and learning

- It supports professional development

- It adheres to organizational standards and policies but is not linked to line management or appraisals

- It is supportive, but it is not counselling.

How does reflective supervision work?

Reflective supervision gives the supervisee the opportunity to stand back from their work. The process of supervision encourages individuals to reflect on and acknowledge the impact work has on them, and with this understanding they are better equipped to objectively analyse their practice to develop and learn from their experiences. A teacher at my own school identified:

Supervision helps me to discuss issues, reflect on my practice and find resolutions.

Psychologist David Kolb developed the 'experiential learning cycle' in 1984 (see Figure 1.2). This cycle has been (and continues to be) used widely in education and psychology to understand how humans learn. Kolb theorized that there were four stages we must go through in order to develop, learn and move forward. This cycle is at the heart of reflective learning.

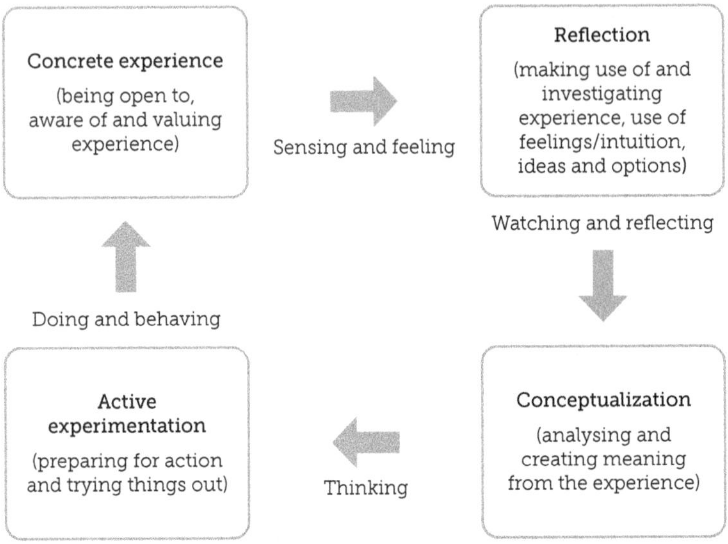

Figure 1.2: Kolb's experiential learning cycle
Source: Billinghurst (2021)

Using the experiential learning cycle for reflective supervision in education

❊ *Concrete experience (sensing and feeling):* The experience stage of the cycle involves information gathering. What happened? Who was directly involved? Who is part of the bigger picture (e.g., other staff members or parents/caregivers)?

❊ *Reflection (watching and reflecting):* The reflective part of the cycle gives staff members the opportunity to think about how they feel about the situation and if those feelings have influenced their decision making in any way. At this stage, it is also important to think about the other people involved, such as pupils, colleagues and parents/caregivers, and how they may be feeling too.

* *Conceptualization (thinking):* Using knowledge from the experience and reflection stages, staff can now use the information to explain what they think is happening. In group supervision, other members of staff can help by sharing their opinions of what they think is happening too. At the thinking stage, it is also useful for both the supervisor and supervisee to draw on knowledge that could deepen understanding of the situation, such as attachment theory.

* *Active experimentation (doing and behaving):* In the final stage, supervisees identify a plan for moving forward. The questions asked by the supervisor, such as 'What are you going to do next?', help staff members to problem solve and come up with their own solutions. This is important as it is not the job of the supervisor to fix the issue or tell the supervisee what to do. Effective supervision supports professional development and gives staff more confidence in their role.

Creating a supervision culture: a whole-school approach

A supervision culture can only be achieved in schools that have a whole-school approach to mental health and wellbeing, a school that recognizes that not all teaching opportunities take place within the curriculum and learning is not only measured through assessments and data. Whole-school learning and development can only take place when we consider the holistic needs of pupils and staff by putting mental health and wellbeing at the centre of education. By providing a safe and compassionate environment, staff and pupils will learn and grow through exploration and reflection. The development of a safe environment encourages mistakes to be viewed as learning opportunities; only then can we achieve our full potential.

In 1943, psychologist Abraham Maslow published his 'hierarchy of needs' in the hope that we could understand, and therefore create, the conditions humans need to reach their full potential (see Figure 1.3).

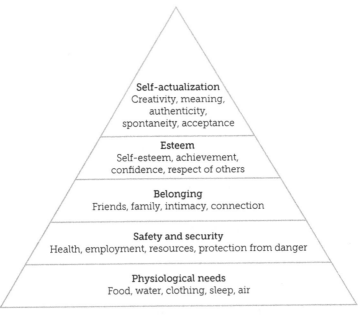

Figure 1.3: Maslow's hierarchy of needs

With a whole-school approach to mental health and wellbeing, schools can provide the ideal learning environment for pupils to reach their full potential. A culture of supervision in schools will help to ensure that staff have the same opportunities.

Supervision and the hierarchy of needs

* *Physiological needs* are met by offering a hot or cold drink (and perhaps a biscuit!). Never underestimate the power of a cup of tea or coffee!

* *Safety and security* is met by ensuring a safe, confidential environment is provided for supervision to take place.

* *Belonging* is met through the supervisory relationship and connections with colleagues (if you offer group supervision).

* *Esteem* can be gained through recognition of achievements, improved confidence and by feeling valued.

* *Self-actualization* can be achieved in supervision as staff are encouraged and supported to achieve their full potential:

  In order for staff to be self-actualized, they must be able to discuss their hopes and dreams for the future with colleagues who genuinely care and want to support them to achieve this. Schools need to have structures in place to have these conversations with staff, and it will lead to happier schools with the potential for staff to flourish and be the best teachers they can be. (Sayer 2021, p.106)

A headteacher's vision, from Melody Kingman, Headteacher, Herne Bay Junior School, Kent

When I took on a headship in September 2017, I knew that a whole-school focus on mental health would be my priority. In the five years leading to my appointment (as deputy head), I had seen a significant rise in the number of children and families who were affected by the social and economic decline within the local community. At the time, there was a greater focus on supporting parents by signposting them to professional and charitable services but, as the impact of rising deprivation took hold within the community, it became clear that increased focus on supporting children with their mental health was required.

Through undertaking the Carnegie Centre of Excellence for Mental Health in Schools Award, we were given a strategic framework to shape and direct our plan. By implementing a whole-school approach we were able to develop practice and influence systemic and sustainable change, leading to our success in achieving the status and recognition of the Gold Award.

Today, our school delivers a shared and embedded vision and culture that drives academic achievement by putting the wellbeing of the children at the heart of teaching and learning. First and foremost, they learn about themselves as young people: how to be and keep safe, how to overcome challenges or difficulties, how to be kind and compassionate and how to work collaboratively and successfully with others. Our teachers and support staff recognize that a child must have a healthy and secure mindset before they can actively approach their learning and make expected progress within the curriculum. My assertion is that 'teaching and learning' and 'mental health and wellbeing' do not and must not sit separately in schools; they are one and the same, an intricate culture that permeates the ethos and environment. We want our young people to recognize and know how to apply themselves when facing or managing difficult or challenging situations, and ultimately, we want them to be successful in achieving their potential.

The undertaking of supervision as a mode of personal and supported reflection is integral to our practice in school. It has become, what I believe to be, a fundamental right of our staff to have access to this practice within their role. How can we expect world-class performance of our school leaders, teachers and support staff unless we invest in their wellbeing and capacity to ensure a safe and trusted learning environment for our children?

By exploring one's attitudes and responses to issues within

a safe and trusted forum, individuals are empowered to seek solutions and make decisions that enable them to more easily manage stressful or challenging situations. As a group, they form a powerful allegiance rooted in respect and they care for one another. Between sessions, they check in despite their busy schedules; the effect of the practice goes beyond the session itself.

I wholly endorse the practice of supervision because I respect the demands on our staff in supporting children beyond the requirement to teach the curriculum. They are professionals in loco parentis: guiding and supporting, loving and caring, knowing and being – they are the first to stand for and protect every child in their care. We, therefore, must protect and provide them with the structure and support to maintain that vital position in the children's lives.

Chapter 1 reflections and planning

* What is your understanding of supervision, and why you would like it in your school?

* What impact would you like supervision to have?

* Do you have a whole-school approach to mental health and wellbeing? If not, what does your school need to work on?

CHAPTER 2

Why Do We Need Supervision in Education?

Working in education is rewarding in so many ways. Those who choose to teach or work in education do so because they are passionate about giving children and young people the best possible start in life. Unfortunately, other factors that are beyond our control sometimes get in the way and make teaching and learning incredibly difficult.

Factors that make teaching and learning more difficult

Mental health

Mental ill health is increasing in children and young people. A recent report from the NHS showed that one in six children aged 6 to 16 were identified as having a probable mental health condition in 2021 – that's five children in every classroom. Schools are now considered a frontline mental health service as the waiting times for assessments in Children and Young People's Mental Health Services can take months, or even years. Anxiety and depression are increasing year-on-year, and behaviours such as self-harm are more common in children and young people than ever before. Supporting the mental health and wellbeing needs of pupils, while balancing the pressures of a packed curriculum, can be challenging for staff to manage, as Geddes highlights:

> The teacher can experience a conflict between concerns about performance and concerns about pastoral care. Little time may be spent on reflecting about how pupils feel. It is worrying to note that often this is expressed in schools as a division of responsibility; between learning and welfare – between cognition and emotion – between practice and progress. Teachers can be focused on curriculum and performance and the pastoral needs of pupils can be the concern of mentors and support staff. This represents the possibility of a significant split in schools' capacities to think about pupils causing concern unless there is a managed policy to bring both aspects of the pupil experience together by discussion and shared thinking. (Geddes 2017, p.139)

Safeguarding

Every year, the updated statutory guidance in the Department for Education's (DfE) *Keeping Children Safe in Education* (KCSIE) contains more safeguarding information for school staff to be aware of. While this is necessary, of course, as safeguarding is the main priority in every school, the increasing safeguarding responsibilities highlight the fact that staff are dealing with issues that can be intense and traumatic for them to manage.

Current guidance in KCSIE states, 'The role of the designated safeguarding lead carries a significant level of responsibility, and they should be given the additional time, funding, training, resources and support they need to carry out the role effectively' (DfE 2022, p.162). While support for the designated safeguarding lead (DSL) is recognized due to the level of accountability and responsibility in their role managing safeguarding in schools, unfortunately, this does not take into account other members of staff who deal with disclosures too:

> Teachers are frequently exposed to potentially distressing and upsetting issues as part of their ever-increasing list of responsibilities. This isn't a bad thing in itself as it means the children feel they have someone to trust in school...however, classroom teachers and support staff are often put in a disclosure situation where students are coming to them with pastoral issues that are distressing in nature, and these have the potential to be upsetting and 'triggering' for the staff member. (Sayer 2021, pp.80–81)

Behaviour

The DfE's *Mental Health and Behaviour in Schools* document was first published in 2014. It contains advice on how schools can promote a culture of positive mental health and includes staff understanding the link between mental health and behaviour. This is certainly more widely understood in education now, and staff recognize that behaviour is a way for children and young people to communicate when they are struggling. However, just having an awareness of this does not make challenging behaviour in a classroom of 30-plus children any easier to manage. Ofsted's *Teacher Well-Being* report (2019, p.7) stated, 'Pupils'/students' behaviour (such as low-level disruption in the classroom, absenteeism, intimidation or verbal abuse) is often a negative influence on teachers' wellbeing at work and will also impact on learning.'

Managing challenging behaviour on a regular basis can impact staff, and 'can cause significant distress to teachers whose work is interrupted, whose skills can be disregarded, and who can feel themselves to be, and sadly sometimes are, attacked' (Geddes 2017, p.128).

Attachment, trauma and Adverse Childhood Experiences (ACEs)

Throughout the DfE's *Teachers' Standards* (2011) it states that positive relationships (between staff and children) are an expectation for teachers. It also states that staff should 'maintain good relationships with pupils', 'develop effective professional relationships with colleagues' and have 'relationships rooted in mutual respect' (2011, pp.12, 13, 10).

Building and maintaining healthy relationships is not always straightforward, however. Early childhood attachments and experiences influence social, emotional and cognitive development. If an infant has an emotionally responsive caregiver, who is attuned to their needs and provides a safe, secure base, they will form a secure attachment. If the caregiver does not, or cannot, provide these things, then the infant will develop an insecure attachment (see Bowlby's attachment theory, 1969). As Geddes highlights, children and young people with insecure attachments will struggle to form healthy relationships at school, and this will present itself in the classroom: 'Some children will have been seriously affected by problematic early relationships, and their behaviour will clearly demonstrate their difficulties in a particular way' (2017, p.65).

Traumatic events, such as Adverse Childhood Experiences (ACEs), also impact attachment, alongside mental and physical health. Some examples of ACEs are:

- Neglect

- Emotional abuse

- Sexual abuse

- Physical abuse

- Domestic abuse

- Bereavement

- Divorce or separation

- Caregiver mental illness

- Caregiver substance abuse.

Research in 2014 found that 47 per cent of people had experienced one ACE, which is almost half of every classroom.

Exposure to ACEs can impact:

- Ability to recognize and manage different emotions

- Capacity to make and keep healthy friendships and other relationships

- Ability to manage behaviour in school settings. (NHS Manchester University 2022)

While it is important that we understand the impact of attachment, trauma and ACEs on children and young people, we cannot forget that adults can still be impacted by their own childhood experiences. The school environment, extreme behaviours and disclosures can re-traumatize staff and impact their mental health, as Sayer describes:

> It can lead to staff suffering from mental and physical ill health and subsequent absences. It can also lead to a relapse in staff members' mental health if they are suffering from PTSD and a child has unintentionally encouraged them to relive their own traumatic experiences by how the child has described them. (2021, p.83)

Workload

Seventy per cent of education staff reported that the volume of workload was the main reason they considered leaving their jobs (Education Support 2021). Ofsted's *Teacher Well-Being* report (2019) found that full-time teachers were working an average of 51 hours each week. The reasons given for this were:

'the volume of administrative tasks, the volume of marking, staff shortages, lack of support from external specialist agencies, challenging behaviour of pupils, changes to external examinations, frequently changing government policies and regulations, and in some cases, lack of skills or training' (2019, p.6). With a heavy workload, it is difficult for staff to have a healthy work–home balance, leading to high levels of stress that can impact their mental health and wellbeing.

What is the cumulative impact on staff?

The increased focus on children's mental health and wellbeing over recent years has been welcomed by schools, although many are falling short when it comes to supporting staff mental health and wellbeing. As a result, teachers and senior leaders are struggling with high levels of stress, which increased further during the COVID-19 pandemic in 2020. The *Teacher Wellbeing Index 2020* (Education Support 2020) showed that nearly two-thirds (62 per cent) of education professionals described themselves as stressed; this increased to 77 per cent for school leaders. By October 2020, new research from Education Support and YouGov found that 84 per cent of teachers and 89 per cent of school leaders considered themselves 'stressed' or 'very stressed', a significant jump from July (2020, p.8). The 2021 figures show that 72 per cent of school staff feel stressed by their work, which is a significant increase on the pre-pandemic figure of 62 per cent.

In an emergency, we are told to put on our own oxygen mask first before helping others; after all, if we don't take care of ourselves, we can't look after those around us effectively. For those working in education, the children always come first – they are the priority. However, if staff mental health and wellbeing is not considered more seriously, and support put in place proactively rather than reactively, higher numbers of staff will reach burn-out. Ultimately, this will lead to more staff being signed off work or even leaving the profession altogether.

Staff retention and absenteeism

Staff retention is an increasing problem in education, with many schools struggling to recruit staff and retain those they already have. The *Teacher Wellbeing Index 2021* (Education Support 2021) states that '54% of staff have considered leaving the sector in the past two years due to pressures on their mental health and wellbeing'.

When staff leave, or are repeatedly absent from work, it impacts school leaders and pupils, and puts additional pressure on the rest of the staff. Staff should, of course, be encouraged to look after themselves if they are unwell, although some repeated absenteeism could be avoided if they were sufficiently supported to manage challenging situations that have the potential to impact them: 'Atkinson (1989) commented that disruptive behaviour has a devastating impact upon teachers that can lead to considerable stress, anxiety and absenteeism within a group of mature, competent, professional people' (Geddes 2017, p.10).

Staff morale

Ofsted's *Teacher Well-Being* report (2019) found that only a small majority of staff felt that school leaders carried out their responsibilities: '57% give praise and recognition for a job well done, 64% help to resolve an issue, when necessary, 52% provide useful feedback and 57% encourage and support their development' (2019, p.46). This means that just under half of teachers feel that leaders are not effectively meeting their own role requirements, and this needs to improve. Ultimately, if staff feel unsupported, yet are expected to meet the standards within their job role consistently, it can lead to less job satisfaction, feeling undervalued and unappreciated. If morale is low, the impact is huge, meaning less engagement and dissatisfaction with work, reduced quality of work, poor communication, negativity and absenteeism.

Poor mental health

Unfortunately, the barriers to reaching out for help in regard to mental health remain in education. Staff with poor mental health may experience:

- Insomnia or difficulty sleeping

- Irritability or mood swings

- Difficulty concentrating

- Over-eating

- Tearfulness

- Forgetfulness

- Muscle tension

- Recurring headaches or migraines

- Dizziness

- Changes to appetite

- Panic attacks

- High blood pressure

- Under-eating. (Education Support 2021)

Thirty-eight per cent of teachers and education staff reported experiencing mental health issues in 2021 (Education Support 2021). More than half (57 per cent) of education staff would not speak to their employer about unmanageable stress or mental health issues. The reasons highlighted were:

- They might be perceived negatively

- It would be seen as a sign of weakness

- The stigma and shame around suffering from mental health issues. (Education Support 2020)

Low wellbeing

In her *Tes Magazine* article 'Wellbeing: Why don't schools offer staff supervision?' teacher Nathalie Downing writes about her experience of feeling emotionally overwhelmed but having nowhere to offload and no one to talk to in school. What are education staff meant to do with the feelings that are stirred up at work?

> I can tell you what we don't do with these feelings; we don't talk about them. Often, we will act them out. We'll let rip at the unsuspecting person at the photocopier when the paper tray has jammed. We'll snap/shout/huff, puff and generally blow the house down around our loved ones. (Downing 2019)

Findings published in the *Teacher Wellbeing Index 2021* (Education Support 2021) showed that 43 per cent of staff do not feel that their organizations support employees who have poor mental health and wellbeing. Recognizing that more needs to be done to prioritize the wellbeing of education staff, the DfE developed *The Education Staff Wellbeing Charter* (2021a). This states that education settings should 'channel support to individuals whose role is known to have a significant emotional component. This might take the form of peer support, supervision, and/or counselling' (DfE 2021a, p.6). While it is positive that this has been recognized, I would argue that it now needs to become a statutory requirement for all education staff, and not just a recommendation.

Outcomes for children

More teachers than ever are suffering with anxiety and depression, stress-related illnesses and burn-out, and we need to consider the impact this has on the children and young people they are teaching. Professionally, teachers are expected to meet consistently high standards; for example, the DfE's *Teachers' Standards* (2011, p.10) state that teachers should 'demonstrate consistently the positive attitudes, values and behaviour which are expected of pupils'. Education staff often feel guilty for not feeling their best, and worry about the impact it could have on their pupils. If school leaders are expecting staff to meet the standards required of them, more needs to done to support their mental health and wellbeing effectively, as a matter of priority. The result of doing so will ultimately benefit the children and young people they teach.

> We firmly believe that children and young people's mental health and wellbeing could be vastly improved if the right support was available for the adults who care for them every day. Levels of stress within the teaching profession mean children and young people are marinating in these stressful environments when they come to school. It's not enough to have staff trained in mental health; if their own cup is empty, how can we expect them to fill up their pupils'? Happy, healthy, regulated children and young people require happy, healthy, regulated adults around them. (Lawrence 2020b, p.11)

Education Support (2021) recommends that schools and colleges:

- Prioritize a culture of wellbeing and reduce stigma

- Look after leadership

- Support staff.

However, they also acknowledge the challenges schools face in regard to finances:

> These recommendations for schools and colleges depend on the availability of sufficient resources. Insufficient funding is one of the drivers of excessive workload, which in turn is a key wellbeing driver. The Government's extra £4.7bn core funding and £1.8bn for education recovery is welcome. However, many schools and colleges still lack sufficient resources to meet the needs of their communities. This is particularly true for smaller schools, and those in areas of increased need. The funding model must evolve again to provide schools and colleges with the capacity to recover, deliver and improve. (Education Support 2021)

Leaders are juggling finances daily and school budgets are already stretched. The areas of most need must be prioritized, but, when considering the facts in front of us, can schools afford *not* to invest in supervision? Ultimately, schools need government support to provide extra funding for the wellbeing of staff and pupils, but until then we must find an achievable way for schools to do this. I believe that the solution is given in this book.

Chapter 2 reflections and planning

* What are your biggest concerns for pupils in your school?

* What are your biggest concerns for staff?

* What could your school do to reduce those concerns?

CHAPTER 3

Who Needs Supervision?

Guidance in the *Statutory Framework for the Early Years Foundation Stage* (EYFS) document states that Early Years teachers should have support within their roles, and Foundation Stage teachers are specifically required to have supervision:

> Providers must put appropriate arrangements in place for the supervision of staff who have contact with children and families. Effective supervision provides support, coaching and training for the practitioner and promotes the interests of children. Supervision should foster a culture of mutual support, teamwork and continuous improvement, which encourages the confidential discussion of sensitive issues. (DfE 2021b, p.26)

The DfE promotes supervision for EYFS teachers as they recognize that it provides staff with the (much-needed) opportunity to discuss concerns related to safeguarding and children's development and wellbeing. The DfE also highlight that supervision offers a space for staff to identify possible solutions and to also improve their personal effectiveness.

Think about the times in your career when you have needed to discuss wellbeing, safeguarding or developmental concerns at school. What role were you doing at the time?

I would argue that *any member of staff* working with children and young people *of any age* should have access to supervision as a means of support and continuing professional development (CPD). Every member of staff in school is responsible for the welfare and progress of the pupils. As explained in Chapter 2, the responsibility for this can have huge implications on staff wellbeing and, subsequently, pupil progress. For that reason, supervision should be accessible for any member of staff coming into contact with children and families.

These are the roles in school to consider for internal supervision:

- Designated safeguarding lead (DSL) and deputy DSL (DDSL)

- Special educational needs coordinator (SENCo)

- Pastoral/inclusion/behaviour roles

- Teachers

- Support staff – teaching assistants (TAs), learning support assistants (LSAs)/1:1's

- Reception staff

- Site staff

- Librarian

- Midday supervisors.

It is worth thinking about staff members who could be exposed to disclosures or those who have difficult conversations regularly, staff such as the librarian or midday supervisors.

This is where it can get complicated, however, depending on the size of the school and the number of staff. It is down to each individual school to work out what is manageable in their setting. Start by prioritizing staff with the most responsibility, such as the DSLs and teachers, and once supervision is established and embedded for those roles, start planning for other staff. Always keep in mind that the aim is for a whole-school culture of supervision.

Supervision for headteachers and senior leaders

You may have noticed that headteachers and the senior leadership team (SLT) were not on this list of staff to consider for internal supervision. This is not because they do not need to have it; it is because it is *essential* that they do, and with an external supervisor.

Figures for senior leader wellbeing in the *Teacher Wellbeing Index 2021* (Education Support 2021) show that 63 per cent have considered leaving the sector in the past two years due to pressures on their mental health and wellbeing, and 80 per cent cited volume of workload as the main reason for thinking about leaving their jobs. The results are shockingly high, yet not surprising. Senior leaders are the foundation of every school. When that foundation is under pressure and not supported, the entire structure is at risk: staff, pupils and their families. Supervision can be the scaffold that supports the whole-school community, starting with the senior leaders to ensure a solid foundation and a whole-school approach to mental health and wellbeing.

The engagement of personal supervision from the SLT is

vital to its success. In order for staff to buy in to supervision, they need to see that the SLT are invested, and benefiting from it too:

> Learning and development are seen as continuous lifelong processes. Thus in such a culture the most experienced and senior staff ensure that they have ongoing supervision or coaching and do not see supervision as just for the untrained and inexperienced. The actions of the senior managers speak louder than their policy statements and it is important that they conspicuously exemplify the learning culture by, amongst other things, having coaching or supervision themselves. (Hawkins and Shohet 2012, p.235)

Talking Heads: External supervision for headteachers and senior leaders, by Lisa Lea Weston, Founder of Talking Heads

Talking Heads was established in 2018 after the seed of an idea had germinated back in 2017 while providing both dramatherapy and supervision in local Devon schools. A throw-away comment by the then head where I worked one day a week in both dramatherapist and supervisor roles had expressed his sadness at wishing for more therapeutic time for his primary children: '...imagine how many more children you could support if you offered that supervision "thing" to headteachers.'

He went on to explain what I absolutely knew to be true: the weight of complexity heads and senior leaders carry, the fact there is so little that can be shared once at home, that it can be overwhelming, exhausting and hard to see the wood for the trees. It is then hard, or impossible, to maintain a balanced ethical objectivity over time, and short-cuts not to be taken end up happening through being ill resourced, both internally and externally. We all seek short-cuts as we get tired. We all start to become the version of who we are when we are ill resourced, and this impacts at every level of our lives, both personal and professional.

Supervision has a long established and ongoing history in social work, midwifery and in psychological therapies and mental health work. I have been in monthly (at least) supervision for 23 years. This is not because I am no good, but because my training taught me that in order to carry on being the best I can be, I need to have a regular, consistent and trusted place to go with all of my confusion and internal build-up, with the complexities that are brought up when working in a service of other human beings. This is not yet part of the culture in education.

Recent years, and with the cutting of budgets across the board for public services, has increasingly meant that schools have had more and more pressure placed on them to be able to not just educate our children but also to hold safeguarding and mental health issues in a way that now has a much broader remit than the days when services were better resourced. For example, the pressures on Children and Young People's Mental Health Services mean that many children are not seen unless they are in extreme distress. Current events and the increased pressures in our society mean that our children are growing up in contexts where parents are less and less resourced with the blessing of time to enjoy the family they have. This is what children need – time and attention, and available, resourced adults at school and home.

Headteachers and senior leaders are repeatedly hearing about safeguarding children in their school. They are repeatedly at risk of vicarious trauma through hearing these stories, being asked to make ethically mature and balanced decisions. Confidentiality means there is nowhere 'safe' to check in or name the times when they themselves are upset by something they hear. Distress often arises from the lack of resources available from other services. I have not had to carry this alone in my career because attending supervision is part of the expectation of my role. Even when I worked in the NHS and supervision was not paid for at times, it was part of my registration expectation with the Health and Care Professions Council, so I attended supervision and funded it privately. I would have done so even if it was not an expectation as I could not work ethically without supervision. Supervision ensures that practice remains challenged and ethical. We all need this, and serious case reviews repeatedly name unchallenged cultures and practice as highly problematic for children and young people, but that supervision as part of a picture may have stopped such events occurring.

While I think supervision is of value and needed in different formats, across the whole school, I decided to focus primarily on one area within Talking Heads. Having been a clinical manager in the NHS I understood absolutely the pressure and split when making a management decision that I had to implement, yet as a clinician serving the clients within the service I ran, I felt it was far from in their best interests. Supervision holds the human beings we work with at the heart of the contracted agreement, but it recognizes that the person in supervision needs deep, safe but challenging support in order to reflect on their work. A safe relationship is needed when moral injury or threat of burn-out is present or over-involvement in an incident. Moral injury, vicarious trauma or burn-out are serious places to reach in terms of capacity to function well for children and young people at work. Supervision cannot often be implemented when someone is in crisis as there is so much shame around when a professional reaches this stage that it can be tough to open up. As James Rielly (a headteacher in a Dorset school and Wessex Association of Leaders in Education (WALE) leader) says:

I don't think I ever really understood the term supervision until

I started to receive it. Because I reached crisis point, the first few sessions were really hard, but as I started to recover, there was less emotion, but always enlightening discussion. To be honest, I wondered that as my emotional state became more stable – about three sessions in – whether I still needed the sessions and even thought maybe Lisa would see me as some sort of charlatan if I didn't reach for the tissues anymore. It took me a while to realize that supervision helps me to 'Lead Happy' and is something that should be compulsory for all heads – in my humble opinion.

James was able to use supervision when in crisis, but it is unusual to be able to do so in a new relationship, and can lead to the supervisee thinking it is only for periods of crisis. A supervisee who begins when they are in a more balanced workplace comes to learn the ebbs and flows of the importance of just regularly going and checking in about how they are at work, each month. They learn then how it catches them at a low point as time goes on, and the shame is easier to deal with because they know their supervisor is safe and they know what they are like in all manner of ways, at work. Supervision is a process and a practice.

I had a strong sense when I began that headteachers not only needed supervision, but I also knew that it was often managers in the NHS (who had no clinical background or who had not had supervision as part of their training) who would take up a position and may try to undermine supervision as they did not see the value. I suspected that providing good regular supervision to heads would mean that they might see the value and roll it out to their senior leadership team (SLT). I hoped it would mean over time the development of a whole-school approach. A cultural change would be occurring along the way where different kinds of conversations would happen. In one school we work with, we began with the head and now see all the SLT between several of us, and the team report that they are braver in their conversations, that as a team they all feel so well supported that they can 'not know' together. If one of them has taken an issue to supervision and says in a safeguarding meeting they have been thinking about the issue in supervision, the rest of the team listen carefully as they know how much work will have gone into the thinking about the child.

Talking Heads began with a pilot of 'free' sessions for eight months to learn how to deliver supervision well, online. This proved a good move given the pandemic! We began with one wonderful assistant headteacher (who we still work with) in a specialist school online. She happened to share this work with Claire Dorer, CEO of the National Association of Independent and Non-Maintained Special Schools (NASS). We began a pilot with 12 NASS leaders for a year, providing monthly supervision. We continue to work with all who remain in the profession: 'The protected space of supervision was particularly valued as a place of sanctuary in which to process, or sometimes just to vent, with a safe person, outside of the structure of the school' (Claire Dorer, personal communication, 2022).

We had also begun with an SLT in London. I was working alone. We have now run year-long pilots for WALE and for St. Christopher's Multi-Academy Trust in Devon. This work is ongoing, and St. Christopher's shared the following:

> The health and wellbeing of staff and children is one of our strategic priorities for us at St. Christopher's Trust; at the end of our year-long supervision trial for headteachers with Talking Heads, 90 per cent of our heads report that supervision is beneficial for them as leaders and that it also benefits the wider staff team, impacting positively on the children in their school. Following the positive outcome of this trial, we are delighted to announce that supervision will continue to be provided for headteachers across St. Christopher's Trust in partnership with Talking Heads.

All the work begun has continued, and three years in we are now working with Education Support providing DfE-funded supervision for up to 272 headteachers, and learning how to keep Gold standard provision, while growing from just me delivering, to three of us in 2019, to there now being over 20 of us delivering supervision through Talking Heads (Education Support n.d.). I have not advertised, but I have engaged in conversations with incredible people on Twitter, a place that terrified me – but I have found that if you try to remain engaged in learning and sharing with others, it is a wonderfully resourcing place. We have grown through word of mouth and, most importantly, we now not only see the head at most of the schools we work with, as quite quickly (as we hoped) sessions are rolled out across the SLT. Several schools we have worked with long term are now working with us to look at a shift in culture within school that allows for supervision and reflective practice for all staff. Again, an SLT that understands through experience and can passionately communicate with their staff what they get from a space where they go to reflect on their work with the children and young people in their school and are professionally vulnerable gives a transformative message and permission to staff that really shifts a culture that has long been based on knowledge, a need to have outcomes and to get it right all the time. But it is in the pause and taking stock that the magic of leadership happens as well as in the classroom.

We know one of the barriers to the SLT accessing supervision is time. We know that, four out of five sessions in, our supervisees wondered how they ever functioned without the space, and that they spend far less time 'worrying' and ruminating because they now have a regular, resourcing safety valve in place. By taking care of our supervisees in sessions and helping regulate their central nervous systems we are helping them take care of their staff, the children and young people, and their own families. A dysregulated adult cannot support other human regulation until they are settled within themselves (Weston 2022).

Moving forward, Talking Heads is offering training with In-Trac Training and Consultancy Ltd. Training is bespoke, and the quality assurance is that any colleagues who do the initial training in supervision remain in external supervision with us so that the educative function can be held. We are making sure that training matches the needs of the children and young people and staff in each setting.

Supervision is beginning to find its way into education. What is vital is that supervision holds firm its principles and that there are skilled and experienced supervisors who can support and 'super-vise' the development of the work. Ultimately super-vision is about ethical work and accountability in the service of other humans. We need to be mindful of it remaining true to its core, and that the people holding such a space are receiving a quality of support themselves. A circle of support is what we need to build in education. We need to collaborate and connect. I truly and passionately believe that for the small 'investment' of one session per month, the outcomes are enormous in terms of impact in relation to the many other hours we may spend where 'little' happens. Supervision always makes a difference if the relationship is good. Supervision in education is ultimately all about the children and young people, but it benefits you too.

Chapter 3 reflections and planning

* What staff will have supervision at your school, and why?

* Start looking for an external supervisor for your headteacher or SLT.

CHAPTER 4

The Benefits of Reflective Supervision

In any organization, the aim is to provide a good service to the service user; in schools, that means the pupils. The welfare and progress of the children and young people is at the heart of every decision made in schools. By offering supervision to staff, schools are recognizing the need to care for the carer. It is an opportunity for staff to charge their batteries and empty their stress buckets, returning to their pupils with a more positive mindset, and feeling better equipped to teach: 'Supervision can at [the] very least allow, albeit briefly, the doors to be shut, the noise to be reduced and a quiet space for satisfying professional conversation' (Davys and Beddoe 2010, p.87).

The personal and professional benefits to supervision will vary in degree depending on the individual. For some, connecting with others will have the most significant benefit. For others, having the time to discuss challenges within their role will have the greatest impact. It is not often (if ever!) that school staff have the time or opportunity to pause and reflect. Supervision offers them time for reflection in a space that also enables them to work through their feelings, acknowledge any challenges, set goals and celebrate successes.

Since introducing supervision in my own school, we have asked the teaching staff to give anonymous feedback regarding their experiences of supervision. Gaining feedback is useful for many reasons (see Chapter 11), and was invaluable when putting together the benefits of reflective supervision in education (see Figure 4.1).

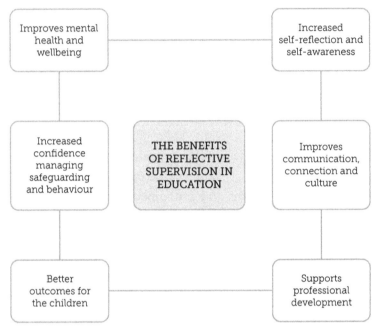

Figure 4.1: The benefits of reflective supervision in education

The benefits of reflective supervision in schools

Improves mental health and wellbeing

Having the opportunity to be open and share thoughts and feelings, in a safe space, can be incredibly cathartic. Schools recognize the importance of emotional regulation for the children, but staff are not given the same opportunities, in an often busy and stressful environment. The *Teacher Wellbeing Index 2021* (Education Support 2021) showed that 72 per cent of school staff are stressed by their work. Supervision allows staff the time to process any stressful and traumatic situations they may have experienced; in the long term, this will reduce the effects of stress on their physical and mental health.

> Think of a time you experienced a stressful or traumatic situation at work. How did you process and work through it?

The most recent data from my own school shows that most staff feel supervision has a positive impact on their mental health and wellbeing (see Figures 4.2 and 4.3).

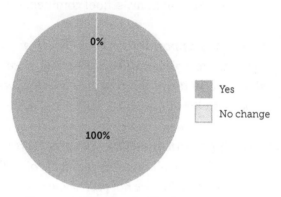

Figure 4.2: Teacher feedback

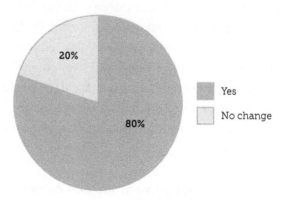

Figure 4.3: Support staff feedback

One member of staff fed back:

> *It provides an opportunity to be more open about how we really feel. It is okay to say 'I'm not okay', which I imagine has been good for everyone's mental health.*

Increased self-reflection and self-awareness

Providing a space for education staff to share their accomplishments, struggles and even moments of uncertainty enables them to focus on their personal strengths and weaknesses. By doing so, they become aware of the skills they have and those that they need to work on or need support with.

A member of staff at my school commented:

> *I think any opportunities to reflect in such a busy profession are so valuable. Reflection is one of the key elements in developing professionally; we can't make progress without it.*

Improves communication, connection and culture

Having the time to talk to other members of staff in schools is rare, particularly if they are not part of your year group or subject team; this can lead to people feeling isolated and disconnected from colleagues. Staff have shared with me that since attending supervision, they feel relieved and reassured to know that others feel the same way they do. Regular, planned supervision ensures individuals do not feel alone, and strengthens a whole-school culture of connection and empathy. Relationships formed in supervision are based on mutual respect and trust.

Feedback from staff highlights how important these relationships are:

> *To have a supportive group and community to rely on is really reassuring.*

I think maintaining empathy is incredibly important and has led to better working relationships.

Teaching can be quite isolating when you're in your classroom; supervision provided a space to connect with colleagues.

Supports professional development

I think most teachers would agree that the bulk of what they learnt about teaching did not come from sitting in a lecture hall at university but by being in a classroom. As mentioned in Chapter 1, we go through stages in order to learn, so while the teaching part is important, so are the reflecting, analysing and planning stages too. Educators often use the 'plan, do, review' cycle in their classrooms as a good way for children to learn, and adults are no different. Reflecting and reviewing practice regularly ensures staff do not become stagnant in their teaching, with a 'one-size-fits-all approach'. A member of staff at my school said:

Supervision has helped me to reflect on my role as a teacher and in school and subsequently helped me to improve both my teaching and classroom management.

It is important that staff have access to CPD throughout their career, but we must remember that it is not the only way to ensure professional development. Supervision provides the opportunity for staff to learn more about themselves, the children and young people they teach, and how best to develop and utilize their skills to deliver the best practice possible:

We cannot rely on the learning we received in our initial training, for the needs of individuals, families, communities and helping organizations are constantly changing and so are expectations and professional best practice. We need to be continually learning, not just new knowledge and skills, but developing our personal capacity, for our own being is the most important resource we all use in our work. (Hawkins and Shohet 2012, p.3)

Better outcomes for the children

Reflective supervision in education is ultimately for the benefit of the pupils. Dysregulated and stressed adults will not be able to provide safety and containment for children. Dysregulated and stressed children will not be able to learn. Supervision provides a space for staff to regulate their emotions in a safe and supportive relationship so they can go back to work and offer children the same thing: happy, regulated adults lead to happy, regulated children. A member of staff at my school recognized that how they 'show up' each day directly impacts the children they teach:

> If I am in a better place, then I have more patience and am more 'present' for the children in my class.

When staff were asked if they felt supervision positively impacted the children, the feedback showed that the majority feel that it does (see Figures 4.4 and 4.5).

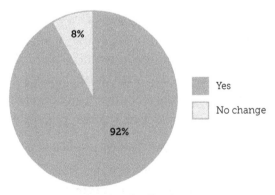

Figure 4.4: Teacher feedback

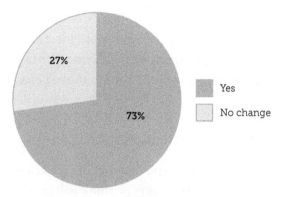

Figure 4.5: Support staff feedback

Increased confidence managing safeguarding and behaviour

Dealing with safeguarding and behaviour are two of the most difficult and emotive aspects of working in schools. Nothing can prepare you emotionally for being spat or sworn at, or for hearing a disclosure of abuse from a child. Training provides staff with the knowledge of what to look out for and the processes to follow, but it can still feel overwhelming and daunting in practice: 'In offering supervision to staff they were given space to feel. This was welcomed and assisted with managing the emotionally demanding aspects of both the teaching role as well as the safeguarding elements within schools' (Sturt and Rowe 2018, p.67).

Sharing worries and talking things through in supervision is beneficial for the member of staff and helps ensure that best practice is followed. Feedback from staff confirmed that they feel supervision has increased their confidence when managing challenging and difficult situations:

Talking through some of the trickier situations that arise in teaching has helped me to manage future situations differently.

Having the opportunities to check in with others and get that reassurance gives me the confidence that I am on the right track in managing some behaviours and reminders of what is behind those behaviours.

Chapter 4 reflections and planning

✳ Considering the benefits of reflective supervision, which of them do you think will benefit your school the most? And why?

CHAPTER 5

The Supervisor

It is important to carefully consider who is best placed to facilitate reflective supervision in school. There are many things to take into account when deciding who is the right person for this role.

The supervisor responsibilities are vast, so organizational skills are essential. They need to have an awareness of school policies and procedures, with a clear understanding of, and training in, safeguarding. They need to be able to keep up-to-date records of sessions, while also taking into account the General Data Protection Regulation (GDPR) and confidentiality.

The key skills required of a supervisor are as follows:

- Organized

- Professional

- Good time management

- Can lead with flexibility

- Good at communicating

- Can manage difficult conversations

- Can abide by confidentiality and its limits

- Can set boundaries – and stick to them!

- A good listener

- Can provide, and receive, feedback

- Knowledge and understanding of supervision.

A basic understanding of counselling skills would be useful. As I have already explained, supervision is not counselling, although the skills used by a counsellor – active listening, reflection and paraphrasing – would also benefit a supervisor.

The personal attributes of the supervisor are also important to consider. Do they show warmth and compassion? Are they empathic? A positive relationship between the supervisor and supervisee is central to effective supervision. The best supervisory relationships are based on trust and respect, and this is created by feeling safe with who you are talking to.

> Think about when you have felt/feel safe. Who/what has helped you to feel that way?

We all know the types of people who make us feel safe. The personality traits required to create that feeling come more naturally to some than others, so it is useful to consider this when choosing a suitable supervisor in your school; supervision will only be effective in a trusting and mutually respectful relationship.

The key attributes required of a supervisor are as follows:

- Compassionate

- Empathic

- Non-judgemental

- Kind

- Trustworthy

- Reflective

- Self-aware

- Good listener

- Reliable.

If you have a member of staff in mind, think about the role they do in school already. Does it align with the role of supervisor? Each school is different, so it would be impossible to say who would be the right person for every school, but there are some roles that complement the role of supervisor. Those to consider are:

- Mental health lead

- DSL/DDSL

- Inclusion lead

- Pastoral lead

- Family liaison officer

- School counsellor

- A member of the SLT.

If you are considering a member of the SLT for the role of supervisor, it is important to think about the dynamics and hierarchy within the relationship. Again, every school is different, and it may be suitable in some schools but not in others. If schools are aiming to create a safe space for staff to be open, then a senior member of staff may not be the right person, although it would be dependent on their job role within the SLT.

Each of the job roles listed already carries a heavy workload, and the person may not have the time and flexibility to add in the role of supervisor. If they are keen to facilitate supervision, and the SLT is committed to embedding it within the school, you will need to discuss this and carefully plan how to make it work.

Finally, you could have someone in mind for the role of supervisor, and they seem to tick all the boxes, but do they *want* to do it? Are they motivated and enthusiastic to be a supervisor? Do they understand what the role involves? For supervision to be an effective and positive experience, it is important that the person facilitating it is keen to do so, and that they have a clear understanding of what it involves.

Understanding the role of a supervisor

For supervision to be effective and worthwhile, the supervisor must understand the role and have a sufficient level of training that qualifies them for the task. In most clinical settings, the supervisor must have a qualification in supervision. In education there is no such requirement, although facilitating reflective supervision does require a level of skill and training. Over the last few years, a few training providers have recognized the need for supervision in education and now offer courses to schools wishing to introduce supervision. The Education People is an example of this as they now run a 'Reflective Supervision Facilitator Training for Schools' course.[1] Leeds Beckett University's Carnegie School of Education and Talking Heads collaborated to create the National Hub for Supervision in Education (NHSE). This 'focuses on providing supervision support/training for teachers and educators whose role involves supporting children and young people with issues affecting their wellbeing/mental health such as stress or anxiety' (Carnegie School of Education 2020, p.5). In-Trac Training and

---

[1]   https://cpdschools.theeducationpeople.org

Consultancy Ltd (2022) have recently developed supervision training for schools too.

If a supervisor is not adequately trained, supervision could cause more harm than good. Barnardo's Scotland published their first discussion paper, *Supporting the Mental Health and Wellbeing of Education Staff Through Professional Supervision Structures*, in 2019. While conducting research for their second paper, *Supervision in Education – Healthier Schools for All*, they identified that poor practice was linked to lack of understanding from the supervisor:

> A common theme was one of lack of understanding or potentially misunderstanding about what Supervision is for – respondents mentioned feeling like the time was more about performance management and less about support, and too much time being spent on practical workload issues rather than the impact this was having on them. They noted Supervisors lacking in understanding or not being sufficiently trained; and that processes felt like a tick box exercise or one in which they were being checked up on. (Lawrence 2020a, p.19)

A motivated supervisor is an effective one

When choosing a supervisor for staff, speak to the person you have in mind before any decisions are made. The most obvious person for the role may not want to do it. Facilitating supervision is a big commitment and involves time, effort and energy from the supervisor, so it is important that they are keen and motivated to take on this important role.

Supervisors must have supervision

In order to facilitate effective supervision, every supervisor must have their own supervision. Personal experience of the supervision process will increase the confidence and knowledge of the person facilitating, and it also ensures good and ethical practice: 'The first step to becoming a skilled supervisor is to receive good supervision. Without this fundamental step the supervisor lacks both a good role model and a solid inner experience of how beneficial supervision can be in one's professional life' (Hawkins and Shohet 2012, p.247).

The acceptance of feedback and challenge

Just as staff need to be challenged and given feedback in supervision, the supervisor must be able to receive it too. Reflective supervision is a collaborative enterprise, and the supervisor is a facilitator, not the expert. Supervisees are encouraged to share their thoughts and feelings in order to reflect on them, so greater awareness and new solutions can emerge, although the thoughts and feelings shared may challenge the supervisor. Ultimately, they must model that learning, and growth can be gained through gentle challenge and constructive feedback:

> It may also be helpful for teachers and supervisors to remember that they are subject to the same group pressures that are influencing their students. In other words, teachers and supervisors are competitive, resistant and reluctant to expose their failures, incompetencies, and insecurities. It is important they should model for their students, not so much perfection which is impossible, but a willingness to learn from their imperfections. (Rioch, Coulter and Weinberger 1976, p.25)

The pros and cons of external supervision

If you do not want to offer internal supervision or you do not have an appropriate member of staff to facilitate it, paying for an external supervisor/s is an option, although there are pros and cons to this approach.

Pro: Different area of expertise

External supervisors can offer a different perspective as their area of professional expertise is outside of education: 'I found it beneficial having someone from another sector who has a different knowledge-base to provide alternative thoughts and ways of thinking...' (Lawrence 2020a, p.13).

Pro: An external supervisor can be impartial

It is easier for an external supervisor to remain impartial in supervision as they are not part of management discussions or impacted by organizational decisions. It is less complicated for the supervisor and (depending on how it is managed) potentially more beneficial for staff. In *Staff Support Groups in the Helping Professions*, Hartley and Kennard report how a facilitator faced a dilemma while running a staff support group within the organization he worked in, when the group he was supporting spoke negatively about a decision made by management. In his position, he had been present during the decision-making conversations and felt that staff had misunderstood the reasons behind it:

> The dilemma was whether I would correct their misunderstanding, or allow them to continue with a discussion and feelings based on what I believed to be erroneous information. It did not seem helpful to me they should feel and act as though they were being badly treated when I did not believe this to be the case. However, I was also reluctant to reinforce an idea of me as being the expert in the group who could provide information and answers that would make everything right. (Hartley and Kennard 2009, p.142)

Con: Expense

School budgets are stretched. With a whole-school approach to mental health and wellbeing, supervision will ideally be offered to all staff who work directly with pupils, so hiring an external supervisor would be costly.

Con: Lack of influence within school

External supervisors have less influence within the school. Where internal supervisors may implement or help shape organizational policies and procedures as part of their role, external supervisors have limited capacity to do so.

Con: Lack of knowledge of school procedures

External supervisors coming in to supervise staff would be unaware of individual school processes or may lack knowledge of how the education system runs in that school. This could impact the process of supervision. A respondent to Barnardo's Scotland's survey about supervision in education shared, 'The occasional difficulty would be around my supervisor not being knowledgeable of the policies and procedures within education so either they couldn't comment or I would spend a lot of the supervision time explaining the processes to them' (Lawrence 2020a, p.13).

Chapter 5 reflections and planning

✻ Do you have a member of staff who would suit the role of supervisor?

✻ What qualities and skills do they have?

✻ What qualities and skills do they lack?

CHAPTER 6

Group and One-to-One Supervision

In this chapter we will look at both one-to-one and group supervision, and the pros and cons for each. It is for individual schools to decide what is best for their setting. It is important to note that you could offer one-to-one supervision to some staff, for example the SENCo or inclusion/pastoral lead, and group supervision to the teachers and support staff.

Group supervision

Most theories suggest that groups go through several stages (see Figure 6.1). It is important to have an awareness of these stages and understand group dynamics if you want to introduce group supervision in your school. In 1965, Bruce Tuckman published his stages of group development, and this has been used in many sectors over the years to get the best out of teams. Sometimes groups work through the first two stages quickly and settle in norming/performing until the group ends. Other groups can spend much longer working through the stages or get stuck; in this case the supervisor will need to use their skills to help the group work through whatever it is that is stopping them from moving forward: 'Groups often return to the earlier stages from time to time, so an understanding of the group dynamics involved is essential throughout the life of the group' (Hawkins and Shohet 2012, p.189).

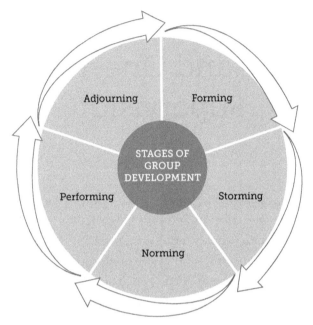

Figure 6.1: Stages of group development

- *Forming:* At the forming stage, group members are getting to know one another. At this point they are often very agreeable and polite to each other. The group can be reliant on the team leader at this stage.

- *Storming:* At this stage, the group can be contentious. Group members feel more comfortable to challenge others, including the supervisor. Some group members may compete with one another or try to prove they are 'better'. At this stage conflict can occur as members behave as individuals and do not work together. A 'storming' group can be difficult to manage, but it is important to remember that it is a normal stage of group development.

- *Norming:* When the group reaches the norming stage, they can work effectively together without little conflict, and if an issue does arise, it can be resolved quickly. The group members understand their roles within the group.

- *Performing:* In the performing stage, the group runs effectively and successfully; this is the stage that groups should spend most time in. Constructive conflict may arise about work, but it does not impact performance. At this stage the group leader is only there to facilitate as the group members can work autonomously.

- *Adjourning:* At the final stage, the group ends. Group members may feel sad, but only for a short time until they join a new group.

Think of a time you have worked in a group. Can you identify the group behaviours at each stage? How did you behave at each one?

Group members leaving and new ones joining

It is important to note that when a group member leaves or a new one joins (including the supervisor), the group will go through these stages again. This may be quick, or it may not – it depends on the group itself.

If new members join a group, there are a few points to consider:

- The new group member may feel excluded and not part of the group

- The group may reject or exclude the new member or compare them to the one who has left

- If the supervisor leaves, the group members may compare them to their replacement and see the new supervisor as 'not good enough'.

Members leaving or new members joining a group can be disruptive and should be avoided if possible, although it is sometimes beyond anyone's control. If it is managed thoughtfully and considerately, it should not cause too many issues. Re-contracting with each new group member is essential and will help to create a safe and cohesive space once again (Chapter 10 explains the importance of contracts).

Advantages to group supervision

There are many advantages to reflective group supervision. Although staff supervision groups are not therapy groups, many of the benefits are the same. Existential psychiatrist Irvin Yalom identified several 'therapeutic factors' in his work with therapy groups (1985), which Hartley and Kennard adapted in *Staff Support Groups in the Helping Professions* (2009, p.47):

- *Catharsis:* Emotional release leading to relief – includes ventilation of feelings, either positive or negative, about life events or other group members.

- *Self-disclosure:* The act of revealing personal information to the group.

- *Learning from interpersonal actions:* The attempt to relate constructively and adaptively within the group, by initiating some behaviour or responding to other group members. More important than other members' reactions is the individual's effort to relate constructively.

- *Universality:* The individual perceives that the other

group members have similar problems and feelings, and this reduces the sense of uniqueness.

- *Acceptance:* The individual has a sense of belonging, being supported, cared for and valued by the group, and of being accepted by others even when revealing something about themselves they had regarded as unacceptable.

- *Altruism:* The person feels better about themselves or learns something positive about themselves through helping other group members.

- *Guidance:* The individual receives useful, factual information or explicit advice and suggestions from the group.

- *Self-understanding:* The person learns something important about their behaviour, assumptions, motivation or unconscious thoughts.

- *Vicarious learning:* The individual experiences something of value for themselves through the observation of other group members.

- *Instillation of hope:* The individual gains a sense of optimism about their own progress or potential for progress in the group.

The feedback from group supervision at my own school has corroborated these findings.

Strengthens connections and relationships

Never underestimate the power of positive relationships. Those who work in schools understand the importance of friendship and acceptance for children – it affects their self-esteem, their confidence, their engagement in the classroom – but it is no different for adults. If staff feel respected and valued for who they are and the job they do, they will thrive:

> *I have felt much more 'in tune' with others in the group and across the school. It has been very reassuring to realize that others share the same concerns and has helped me to feel more secure in my own judgements of situations.*

For trusting relationships to be established, ensuring safety early on in the group is vital and can be created with a thorough and clear contract during the first session (see Chapter 10). A teacher at my own school recognized the importance of this as it enabled them to open up more easily:

> *I think this group established mutual respect early on and this helped people to be honest. It was nice to not feel judged.*

Shared experiences

Groups can provide support in what can be an isolating role. Group supervision provides an opportunity for staff to recognize that others are facing, or have dealt with, similar issues. Staff have limited opportunities to interact with one another in the busyness of the school day. When staff first came together for supervision in my own school, they became consciously aware and were able to acknowledge how disconnected they felt to one another. A teacher in my own school found that supervision provided the space and time for staff to connect at a different level:

> *Group supervision helped to build a sense of 'togeth-erness', because it was a forum to recognize that we're facing similar/or had faced similar challenges and that*

was very supportive – in terms of both other individuals helping me to reach a point of clarity or helping other individuals in the group to reach that point themselves.

Shared knowledge

Shared knowledge and different perspectives are big advantages to group supervision. Staff can sometimes fall into the trap of believing they have tried everything or that nothing will help. By sharing with others in the same role, it is possible to gain new insights from the knowledge of others. Group supervision is particularly beneficial for early career teachers (ECTs) if they are in a group with more experienced teachers. Equally, ECTs can bring fresh approaches and ideas to the metaphorical table, and this can be enlightening for staff who have been teaching for a long time:

I've enjoyed listening to different points of view; this has been enriching for me. I have become much more convinced by the importance of good communication and the possibilities that this brings.

You can reach more people

For practical reasons, group supervision enables the supervisor to reach more staff at one time. Education settings vary in size considerably, and this will impact how each school will choose to run supervision, alongside other considerations. As Hawkins and Shohet (2012) point out, some of the reasons organizations opt for group supervision 'may be connected to economics of time, money or expertise. Clearly if there is a shortage of people who can supervise, or their time is very limited, supervisors can probably see more supervisees by conducting supervision groups' (2012, p.178). They point out, however, that the decision to offer group supervision should come from a positive choice, not because there is no other option.

Disadvantages to group supervision
Group dynamics and personalities
Group dynamics and different personalities can bring up issues in group supervision. Although it can be managed with the facilitation of a skilled supervisor, it may affect the participation of group members. One teacher felt that due to different personalities in their group, they weren't as open:

> *There have been times where I have sometimes wanted to speak up about things but potentially felt that I couldn't...not because I didn't feel that it was a safe space but more of it being a personal barrier to open up to people that I am quite different to.*

Conflict
While some conflict is perfectly normal during all group stages, it can cause anxiety for some. Again, if managed appropriately by the supervisor, it should not cause any lasting problems. It is useful for the supervisor to explain the group stages of development to the group, so they feel reassured that it is part of the process, rather than there being an issue with the group:

> *I think we are a group that really work well together. I think we're lucky because of that. I don't know how it would work if we were a different group of people.*

Vulnerability
Revealing professional challenges and the feelings they evoke can make staff feel vulnerable. If you decide that supervision is to be mandatory in your school (more on this in Chapter 8) and you are going to run it in groups, it is important that staff have a clear understanding of what's involved and the boundaries in place to keep them safe (explained further in Chapter 10).

In some cases, it may be beneficial to offer one or two one-to-one sessions first.

A member of staff in my own school shared:

> *My feelings are very personal and I don't necessarily feel comfortable to share them with a group. I feel better one-to-one with a trusted person.*

One-to-one supervision

We will now look at the advantages and disadvantages of one-to-one supervision.

Advantages

Tailored to individual needs

One-to-one supervision is tailored to the need of the individual staff member and can therefore go wherever it needs to, within the session. This can lead to a deeper understanding and greater self-awareness for the supervisee. A member of staff at my own school felt that one-to-one supervision offered support at a pivotal point in their career, when they were changing roles:

> *Attending supervision last year was helpful in supporting my development in my new role. Supervision allowed the opportunity to work through the more emotional/psychological challenges of a new role. I'd had mentors, but I would consult them more on the operational challenges – how to do the role and my impact on the role. Supervision was an opportunity to work through how that role was going/the role's impact on me, without a loss of confidence in the role I was doing. I found it useful to have that separation – two distinct places to work through those two aspects.*

No holding back

With only the supervisor listening, supervisees may be more open and willing to share their challenges or weaknesses; they may not worry so much about saying 'I need to work on that'. At my school, a member of staff fed back:

> *With individual supervision, it was beneficial to have a space and more time to reflect on a new role and its impact on me with little experience in that role without a loss of confidence or fear of judgement from peers or line managers.*

More time

It goes without saying that one-to-one supervision offers individual staff more time, and, therefore, more opportunity, to reflect and develop in their role. The time is shared among the group members in group supervision, so staff, and the supervisor, need to be more focused on the agenda items; one-to-one supervision offers more flexibility.

Disadvantages

The disadvantages to one-to-one supervision are those identified as positives for group supervision:

- No opportunity to build connections and relationships with colleagues

- No opportunity for colleagues to share their experience or knowledge

- It is more time-consuming for the supervisor, and therefore limits the capacity for a whole-school approach.

Chapter 6 reflections and planning

* Will you offer group or one-to-one supervision, or a mixture of both?

* Why did you make that choice?

CHAPTER 7

The Supervisory Environment

It is often the case that if you need a space in school (that isn't a classroom!), you have to make do with wherever is available. Space is a precious commodity in schools, so every nook, cranny and corridor is utilized. This is workable for the most part, but it is not appropriate for supervision.

Providing the correct supervisory environment is key to effective supervision, hence why there is a whole chapter dedicated to this topic. Finding the right space for supervision will take time and planning. There are many 'ideals' that we would hope to achieve, but there are some that are non-negotiable.

The three C's

There are *three key elements* to the supervisory environment that schools must take into account when planning supervision for staff:

1. *Confidentiality:* It must be a safe space for staff. If supervisees feel they are going to be overheard by others in school, they will not feel able to speak openly.

2. *Comfort:* Staff attending supervision need to be free from distractions during the session. Place a 'Do not disturb'

sign on the door and turn all phones to silent. From a practical point of view, it is also important that staff are comfortable enough to be able to sit for a considerable amount of time.

3. *Consistency:* Find a room that can be used for each session. Trust and safety will be established more quickly in an environment that is familiar.

Table 7.1 gives a clear idea of what you should be aiming to achieve and the things to bear in mind when finding a space for supervision to take place.

Table 7.1: The supervisory environment

Must haves	No-no's	Ideals
• Confidential, private space • Comfortable room with no distractions • Consistent room that is available for every session	• Staff room, corridor, walk-through room, an office being used by other staff • Ringing phones, knocks at the door, uncomfortable seating • A regular change of room, with no forewarning	• Empty office, classroom, library or hall • Facilities to provide a hot/cold drink • A designated, protected space

By providing a space for supervision that is confidential, comfortable and consistent, staff will feel safe and valued, allowing them to achieve the greatest benefits possible. Ensuring a protected space for supervision also highlights its importance. Finding a designated supervision space may be a challenge, but it communicates to staff that it is a priority, and will help to promote a positive supervision culture in school.

When teachers at my own school were asked what they

valued about supervision, it was noted that the environment contributed positively to their experience:

> *The chance to talk through things in a calm and warm environment.*

> *Being able to escape somewhere different and neutral.*

If you are considering offering online supervision, the three C's still need to be considered. However, finding a confidential space is down to the supervisee(s) and would need to be discussed with them when contracting for the sessions (see Chapter 10).

Online supervision

In professions where supervision is commonplace, online supervision was not widely practised before the COVID-19 pandemic. When schools closed during the first lockdown, it seemed inevitable that supervision would stop due to its relational nature. However, many professionals (including supervisors) were suddenly expected to do their job effectively online. All meetings that had previously been carried out face-to-face now took place virtually, as it was the only option – and it was better than nothing at all! One of the biggest losses during the pandemic was connection with others: family, friends and colleagues. Supervision became the ideal space to keep staff connected, even if it was online. But was it as ineffective as we feared it might be?

In the 2019/20 end-of-year review, teachers at my own school were asked how useful they had found the virtual supervision sessions. Somewhat surprisingly, the results showed that the vast majority found online sessions were equally as useful as face-to-face sessions (see Figure 7.1).

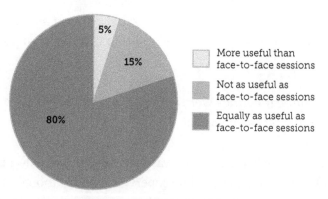

Figure 7.1: Online supervision

When offered the opportunity to add additional comments, it was evident that staff opinions varied based on their own personal situations and how confident they felt using technology. Some valued supervision for entirely different reasons during lockdown, and recognized that, at that time, they appreciated the supportive element of it more:

> *I have clicked 'More useful' simply because the supervision was really essential at the point that we were in lockdown. We dealt with tougher issues and more personal anxieties.*

> *I think that meeting online perhaps had an effect of allowing people to open up more, even though we might have expected the opposite. I'm not sure if that's true or if it's just that the sessions have felt increasingly relevant during COVID times. I also think that we listened better because of the logistical aspect of muting and unmuting.*

Other feedback suggested that while the virtual sessions were useful, staff found it more difficult to communicate online:

I think the online were nearly just as good as the face-to-face sessions, but it is easier to interact with people in real life.

Online meetings were as useful, but I didn't like them. It didn't feel as personal.

What the feedback did show was that there are both advantages and disadvantages to online supervision and, although it was considered equally as beneficial to most people, face-to-face was preferred, if given the option (see Table 7.2).

Table 7.2: Advantages and disadvantages to online supervision

Advantages	Disadvantages
• You can join wherever you are	• Technology issues
• Mitigates the spread of viruses	• Not as personal
• You can still attend when not at work (if you choose to)	• It is harder to maintain focus on a screen
	• Can be difficult to find a quiet, confidential space

It is important to bear in mind that supervision had already been established face-to-face when we moved to online supervision during lockdown. During those early face-to-face sessions, we built a trusting relationship that helped to support the move to online supervision. If that had not been the case, the results may have been different.

Chapter 7 reflections and planning

＊ Do you have a space in mind for supervision?

＊ Does it meet all the criteria? If not, how will you ensure the three C's are achieved?

＊ Would you consider offering online supervision for your staff? Reflecting on your answer, why do you think that is?

CHAPTER 8

Setting Up Supervision in Schools

Once you have reached the stage of setting up supervision, your school should have already:

- Identified a suitable supervisor who is motivated to do the role

- Found an appropriate space for supervision to take place

- Decided if you will be offering one-to-one or group sessions, or a mixture of both.

With these key elements in place, you can now think about the practical aspects of supervision that need to be decided on before you introduce it to staff. Setting up supervision in schools is not a simple task, but it is important to get this stage right for supervision to be effective, supportive and long lasting. In her *Tes Magazine* article, Downing writes, 'There are challenges to setting up these groups, but investing in the wellbeing of the adults in school enables them to be emotionally lighter and have greater capacity to support and teach the children in their care' (2019). It is important to keep this in mind when setting up supervision, especially if there are obstacles along the way.

Name

You may feel that 'supervision', or 'reflective supervision', is not the right name for your school. It is important to bear in mind that if supervision is explained properly to staff and they understand its purpose, then the name does not really matter. Equally, if you deliver effective supervision, then calling it something else does not change its functions or benefits. As Shakespeare said in *Romeo and Juliet*, 'What's in a name?' (2000).

Other suggestions for 'supervision' are:

- Wellbeing sessions/groups

- Staff support sessions/groups

- Reflective practice sessions/groups.

Frequency

The frequency of sessions will depend on other factors: the needs of the school, the availability of the supervisor, the number of staff, class cover and if you will be offering one-to-one or group sessions.

Ideally staff should attend supervision monthly, but when taking into account other considerations, this may not be possible. For supervision to be effective and beneficial, it must take place at least once a term so that staff attend a minimum of six sessions over a school year.

Length of sessions

The length of supervision would, again, depend on other factors, the most important one being if you are planning one-to-one or group sessions. If you decide to offer group supervision, then you would need *up to 2 hours*. If there are three to four people in a group, then 1.5 hours would suffice; any more members than that and you would need the full 2 hours.

If you are planning to offer one-to-one sessions, then each session should be a minimum of 1 hour; any less than that would be a rush.

Group size

If you decide to offer group supervision sessions, you need to think about the size of the groups. This will vary depending on how many staff are having supervision and how much availability the supervisor has. The minimum number in each group would be three and the maximum would be five; if the group was larger it would be difficult for the supervisor to facilitate, and there would not be an adequate amount of time available for each staff member.

Group mix

The members of each group should have the same, or similar, job roles, for example teachers, TAs/LSAs/1:1's, pastoral/inclusion/behaviour roles or DSLs. This is useful during supervision as they will have shared experiences and knowledge to draw on. It will also help to reduce issues with hierarchy.

When planning supervision for teaching staff, it is beneficial to mix up year teams (in primary schools) and subject teams (in secondary schools). This is helpful for a few reasons:

- It creates connections and builds relationships with different members of staff

- They will bring different experiences and insights from their own year groups or subjects

- It gives staff an opportunity to discuss any challenges or issues in their own year groups or subjects.

Time of sessions

The time of the sessions themselves doesn't really matter, although it is necessary to give staff process time after each one so they can achieve the greatest benefit from supervision. Reflection of the session should continue after it as much as it does during it; going straight back to work or into a class is not ideal and would be detrimental to what your school is trying to achieve. If sessions come to an end once school has already finished, staff have the option to go straight home if they would like to, but, most importantly, they do not have to go back to a busy classroom or work environment.

In my own school, we decided that supervision for teachers would start during the school day and end after school. It was important to us that supervision did not finish too late (staff have other commitments and family lives), but we also needed to be practical when thinking about cover for their classes. For my school, this means group sessions are held at 2.30–4pm; 45 minutes of class time is covered by a TA and the 45 minutes remaining is after school. This has worked well over the last three years, without causing any major issues. If your school cannot make this (or something similar) work, I would suggest that you arrange for staff to have a short break (of 10–15 minutes) after their session.

Booking in the sessions

How you book the sessions in would depend on who is having supervision and if you are booking in one-to-one or group sessions, as it comes down to flexibility and availability. For example, if you were booking in one-to-one sessions with a non-teaching member of staff (such as a pastoral lead), you could choose to book in one session at a time. If the member of staff has a teaching responsibility, they may not have as much flexibility, and cover would also need to be organized. For the benefit of the whole school, I have found it useful to book in all sessions (Terms 1–6) at the start of the year; I do this with all group and one-to-one sessions. At the beginning of each school year (once I have established how many groups and individual supervisees I have), I go through the school diary and book in every session for the year ahead – as you can probably imagine, this is a big job! It takes patience, organization and communication, but once it is done, the benefits make it a worthwhile task. Everyone involved puts the sessions in their diary to ensure no other meetings or events are booked in and cover can be organized well in advance. Once I have completed the supervision timetable, I always give staff an opportunity to come back to me with any issues or clashes that I might not be aware of; that way any changes can be made early on.

It is important to share the supervision timetable with all staff who may need to know, not just the person/people attending. Those to consider are:

- The SLT
- Reception/office staff
- Cover supervisors
- Year group leads/heads of departments
- Line managers
- Teachers (if the supervisee is a TA or 1:1 in their class)
- TAs (if they cover the class for a teacher).

Good communication will make all the difference and enable supervision to run smoothly; the last thing you want to do is cause stress and anxiety for others. It's important to keep in mind that you want to create a positive supervision culture within your school.

Finally, once the supervision sessions have been booked in, and agreed by staff, the dates cannot be changed unless it is *absolutely* necessary (particularly with group supervision as it impacts more than one person). It is crucial that supervision takes precedence over anything else that crops up through the year. Why? Because other things *always* come up in schools. There will always be another meeting, more training, a school trip you need to support with, and so on. It will take time and dedication to embed supervision in schools that have not used it before. To start with, staff will be unsure of what to expect, may try to avoid going or not understand its importance, so it is paramount that school leaders show their commitment to staff. By prioritizing supervision, you are showing staff that you are prioritizing *them and their wellbeing.* By offering regular and planned opportunities to speak openly, and by encouraging them to talk through professional challenges and difficult experiences, staff will feel supported and have a greater sense of togetherness:

> Isolation can cause a great deal of work stress if someone feels that they are carrying something on their own. For school staff who are dealing with stressful circumstances around the needs of children and young people, isolation can compound this feeling. In this way, *regular, planned* supervision can play a role in ensuring that staff have appropriate support. (Anna Freud National Centre for Children and Families 2020, p.10; emphasis added)

Mandatory or optional supervision

There are pros and cons for offering either mandatory or optional supervision to staff, and you will need to decide which one will work best in your school. There are several points to consider when making this decision.

Mandatory supervision

This ensures everyone attends (for example, all the teachers).

Pros

This is the best way to ensure a whole-school approach to supervision and means the greatest possible number of staff will experience its benefits. People who have not experienced supervision before may not want to attend (see Chapter 9) and, if given the option, will choose not to go. A teacher at my own school said:

> *When I was first told about supervision, I didn't want to take part in it. To me, it didn't seem necessary. It being compulsory made me go and I really benefited from the sessions.*

Cons

Stipulating that everyone must attend supervision could create resentment if there are members of staff who do not want to attend. To ensure this does not happen, the reasoning behind your decision needs to be explained clearly and thoughtfully when introducing supervision to staff.

If a member of staff shares that they feel anxious or vulnerable attending supervision, they should be listened to and supported appropriately. It may be useful to offer some one-to-one sessions first (if you are organizing group sessions) so they get a feel for what it is like. The benefits of attending supervision will become apparent to them soon enough, but their well-being must be considered if the idea of supervision is causing them distress. This would need to be managed carefully and thoughtfully by the supervisor and, if appropriate, their line manager or the headteacher.

Optional supervision

This gives staff the choice to attend supervision.

Pros

For some schools, giving staff the option to attend supervision could mean that they can offer it out to more people within school; for example, if only half of the teachers choose to attend, then there is more availability for support staff to attend.

Cons

If supervision is optional to staff, those who need the support most may not attend. If feeling overwhelmed or stressed, it is unlikely staff will want to commit to something else, especially if given the option.

Staff who do choose to attend supervision may feel guilty for doing so due to workload pressures on them and the fact that other members of staff are not going.

Staff who have chosen not to attend supervision may later change their minds, and it may no longer be possible to accommodate them. You will need to bear this in mind, and have a protocol in place, should this happen. Good planning and communication when introducing it to staff will help.

If you choose to run group supervision sessions and make them optional, I suggest that you ask those that want to attend to make a commitment and then stick to the groups you have set up. While it may work for your school to give staff the choice to attend supervision, it would be disruptive if people attended some sessions but not others. It would also be unsettling if new staff joined once the group was established, although this is unavoidable at times and can be managed (as explained in Chapter 6).

Chapter 8 reflections and planning

✻ What will be the barriers to setting up supervision in your school?

✻ Will supervision be mandatory or optional? Why?

CHAPTER 9

Introducing Reflective Supervision to Staff

Before introducing reflective supervision to staff, your school should have:

- A leadership commitment to supervision

- A member of staff committed and adequately trained to be the school supervisor

- External supervisors for the headteacher/SLT and school supervisor.

For staff to value and recognize the importance of supervision, it must be introduced with all staff (who are being offered supervision) in attendance alongside the headteacher, the senior leaders and the supervisor – for staff to buy in to it they will need to see that supervision is a priority for school leaders. I would recommend setting up a staff meeting to introduce it so you have *at least* an hour to go through the main points, and then staff can be given the opportunity to ask questions.

It is important that staff understand the rationale behind supervision and the benefits of having it. It is unlikely that many of them will have heard of supervision before, let alone experienced it, so explaining it clearly and concisely is key. The school leadership and the supervisor must be prepared to answer any questions; if they are unclear of the process in any way, then it could cause confusion or anxiety for staff. In their second discussion paper *Supervision in Education – Healthier Schools for All*, Barnardo's Scotland found that 'respondents who shared negative experiences highlighted issues around lack of clarity about what the sessions were for' (Lawrence 2020a, p.13).

The key pieces of information I recommend you include when introducing reflective supervision to staff are:

- Introduce the supervisor and give details of the training they have had to do the role.

- The three functions of reflective supervision: normative, formative and restorative (Proctor 2008). It would be useful to show staff Proctor's diagram (Figure 1.1) to explain each of the functions.

- Kolb's experiential learning cycle (1984): concrete experience (thinking), reflective observation (reflecting), abstract conceptualization (conceptualizing) and active experimentation (planning and doing). Again, it would be beneficial to show staff Figure 1.2, and explain the stages of the learning cycle.

- Maslow's hierarchy of needs ([1943] 2013): physiological needs, safety and security, belonging, esteem and self-actualization. Using Figure 1.3, explain how supervision can meet these needs.

- Explain how supervision will run in your school, using your reflections and planning from Chapters 6–8.

Key things to mention at this stage are:

- *Confidentiality:* This is most likely going to be one of the biggest concerns for staff who are new to supervision.

It would be helpful to explain the contract, and the purpose of it, to reassure staff that discussions that take place during supervision remain confidential, apart from the exceptions (see Chapter 10).

- *The difference between supervision and counselling:* It is important that staff understand that supervision is *not* counselling. You will have already explained the functions of reflective supervision so they will have an awareness of its supportive nature; however, it is imperative that staff are aware that supervision is a space to discuss *work* and the feelings that arise in their professional role. This may be confusing to begin with and might only become clear once staff have attended one or two sessions and experienced it for themselves. After attending their first three sessions (as part of the mid-year review, explained in Chapter 11), staff at my school were asked what their expectations had been of supervision before it started. One supervisee said:

I wasn't sure what to expect really, but I guess I had the image of lying on a couch with a psychiatrist in mind!

This could cause anxiety for some people, so make sure you reassure them that they are not attending supervision to be analysed!

- *Staff only have to share what they feel comfortable with in supervision:* Supervision will be an alien concept to people who have not experienced it. The idea of sharing your thoughts, feelings and struggles with people you work with (either the supervisor or colleagues in group supervision) may be worrying to some, especially those who do not naturally share with others. The thought of supervision could leave some staff feeling vulnerable or exposed: 'Members need to be sure that their privacy will not be invaded and that the group will not venture into areas that will undermine the capacity of colleagues to work together' (Hartley and Kennard 2009, p.29).

- *And finally, give staff the opportunity to ask questions, give feedback or share any concerns they might have:* Staff must be given the time to ask questions and share concerns. A common concern at my school was time pressures and 'fitting something else in'. This is understandable, and I found it helpful to remind staff that it is only 1.5 hours, once a term (minimum), and the benefits to be gained from it far exceed the time put across to it. Interestingly, the feedback I get from staff now is that supervision needs to be more often!

At this stage, I found it useful for staff to hear my own experiences of supervision as it showed my commitment to the process too. If staff feel that the school leadership are invested in it, then the culture of supervision will be a positive one. In *Best Practice in Professional Supervision*, Davys and Beddoe identified that: 'Workplace cultures can exert positive and negative influences on the attitudes of staff and their motivation to participate fully in learning activities, including supervision' (2010, p.73).

Developing a supervision policy

Every school must develop a supervision policy that suits the needs of their school and clearly lays out the purpose and aims of supervision. The policy should be in place before supervision commences and should be shared with staff.

Using the reflections and planning from previous chapters and the feedback you have from staff regarding what they feel they need in their role (either through a staff survey (Chapter 11) or through discussions), the leadership team and supervisor must develop a reflective supervision policy that fits with their school and staff.

I have developed a policy that can be used as a starting point for schools. It is important that each school has a supervision policy that is meaningful to them. The template on the following pages is just to be used as a guide.

REFLECTIVE SUPERVISION POLICY

Appropriate self-evaluation, reflection and professional development activity is critical to improving teachers' practice at all career stages. (DfE 2011, p.7)

Policy statement

Good supervision can give staff an opportunity to reflect on their practice, explore any worries or concerns they may have about the welfare and development of all children in the setting and contribute towards highly effective practice and increased staff confidence. This supports the development of a safe setting where children are safeguarded from harm. In addition, good supervision can support staff wellbeing.

[THE SCHOOL NAME] are committed to ensuring that members of staff receive good quality effective supervision on a regular basis. Reflective supervision is offered to newly qualified and experienced staff. This policy sets out the expectations of how staff should be supervised and guides leaders in the key elements needed to ensure staff are supervised effectively.

Supervision aims:

- The culture of the setting is embedded

- There is a whole-school approach to mental health and wellbeing

- All staff are respectful to one another

- All staff are respectful to every child

- Staff can discuss good and poor practice

- Staff feel safe to discuss their own mental health and wellbeing

- Staff are confident and feel supported in managing safe-guarding concerns

- Children are listened to

- Staff are listened to

- Staff feel valued

- Staff can challenge poor practice

- Whistleblowing procedures are in place and staff know how to use them.

What is supervision?

Supervision is an important part of staff wellbeing, development and in keeping children safe. At **[THE SCHOOL NAME]** we recognize its importance and value, so therefore we provide supervision to all staff with a responsibility for children.

Using the adult learning model, supervision should provide opportunities for staff and the supervisor to:

- Discuss and challenge concerns, issues or difficulties

- Review and reflect on work-related issues

- Explore feelings and emotional impact or work

- Explore the understanding of school policy, philosophy and practice

- Ensure every child's safety and wellbeing

- Develop practice and competencies, including training needs

- Identify solutions to address concerns and issues

- Take away ideas/solutions/plans for moving forward.

At **[THE SCHOOL NAME]** supervision has three functions

– educative, supportive and managerial – to ensure that it meets the needs of the children, staff and the school.

What are the benefits of supervision?

The main beneficiary of supervision should be the service user, so in the case of **[THE SCHOOL NAME]**, this means the children who attend the school.

Effective supervision ensures the delivery of efficient and safe care through regular discussion, reflection and professional support; staff may also recognize areas they need training in or support with. Supervision has been found to support increased staff retention, which ensures continuity of care for the children.

For the member of staff (the supervisee), supervision provides professional support and a safe space to discuss and reflect on their professional role, workload, concerns and successes. The supervisory relationship is based on trust, which allows for free and open discussion and learning without the fear of being criticized. Employees should receive constructive feedback about their work, with concerns being challenged sensitively and honestly, and successes being acknowledged on a regular basis. This hopefully increases the feeling of being valued by the school, which, in turn, increases job satisfaction and improves wellbeing.

Effective supervision encourages motivated, confident employees who understand the principles of safe practice so they can support each other more effectively in school. Supervisees are more focused and communication between staff is improved, which increases productivity.

The qualities of a good supervisor

Supervision is only effective and positive for individuals and the school if it is carried out by the 'right' person. Supervisors should be extremely competent, have a degree of leadership skills and have received adequate training to ensure good and ethical practice. They need to be clear about their role and responsibilities and have their own external supervision.

Some of the skills of a 'good' supervisor are:

- Organized

- Professional

- Good time management

- Can lead with flexibility

- Good at communicating

- Can manage difficult conversations

- Can abide by confidentiality (and its limits)

- Can set boundaries and stick to them

- Has good listening skills

- Can provide, and receive, constructive feedback.

The rights and responsibilities of the supervisees:

- To receive effective and sensitive supervision

- To be treated in an anti-discriminatory manner

- To have their feelings and opinions recognized

- To raise issues of concern about their own practice and that of their colleagues

- To learn from mistakes and seek advice if they are unsure

- To be listened to and receive appropriate professional support

- To commit to regular supervision and understand its value.

The contract

At **[THE SCHOOL NAME]**, we believe that it is essential that supervisors and supervisees jointly develop a supervision contract before supervision is undertaken. The contract is annotated and agreed at the first one-to-one or group supervision session.

Confidentiality

It is important for staff to be comfortable in discussing all aspects of their work, but there needs to be clarity as to what will happen to information discussed if it raises concerns about the practice of a particular member of staff or a child. Accordingly, any supervision policy must be compatible with the safeguarding children, allegations against staff and confidentiality policies within the school. Any records agreed through the supervision contract should be maintained confidentially and not be accessible to other school staff.

Frequency and length of sessions

Staff attend supervision once every term amounting to six sessions over the school year. The sessions are booked in advance and shared with staff with plenty of notice.

The sessions are between 1 and 1.5 hours in length. If attending group supervision and the group has more than four members of staff, it will increase to 2 hours.

One-to-one and group supervision

One-to-one: Staff identified by the supervisor and the leadership team will be offered one-to-one supervision sessions.

Group: Staff identified by the supervisor and the leadership team will be offered group supervision sessions. Year group/subject teams will be mixed up.

Reviews and feedback

All staff attending supervision will be required to complete twice-yearly reviews to enable the school to evaluate its effectiveness and gain staff feedback. All staff feedback will be anonymous.

Reporting concerns

If a member of staff has concerns regarding supervision, they are encouraged to share these with their supervisor. If unable to, staff can speak to the headteacher.

Lead members of staff:

- Supervisor:

- Headteacher:

Policy review

This policy will be reviewed annually. The review date is:

Chapter 9 reflections and planning

✻ Start thinking about your reflective supervision policy. What does your school need to have in it?

CHAPTER 10

The Content of the Sessions

Those of you who are completely new to reflective supervision in education might be wondering what a session would look like. There is no script to follow, as the session content is dependent on what the supervisee brings to the sessions; however, there are certain things that must be covered initially, and a format that can be followed each session thereafter.

Session one: the contract

Supervision must begin with a clear contract (or working agreement, if you would prefer) that has been negotiated by the supervisor and supervisee(s). The contract is created by all parties involved and should reflect the expectations of the supervisor, supervisee and the school; it can take the form of a verbal or written agreement.

The contract ensures the following:

- The *practicalities* are discussed

- The *boundaries* are clear

- *Confidentiality* and its limits are understood and agreed to

- The *session structure* is explained.

Practicalities

- *The time of each session and the importance of punctuality:* On occasion, supervisees may be held up in class, or they may need to leave early if they have a family commitment outside of school. In these (or similar) situations, communication is required.

- *Where supervision will be held:* Ensure that those attending supervision are clear as to where it will be held.

- *Supervisees' phones:* If supervisees bring their mobile phones with them, they must be switched off or on silent and put away so as not to distract anyone. If they need to keep it on for any reason (such as waiting for an important phone call), they must make everyone present aware.

- *Absence:* The supervisor and supervisees must agree how best to communicate if anyone is absent on the day of a session.

- *Respect:* All parties must treat each other, and other members of the school, with respect at all times. To create a safe, open space, everyone involved must feel valued and respected. In group supervision it is normal for supervisees to have different opinions and experiences, although supervision should be a place to share and discuss them professionally and respectfully.

- *Participation:* For supervision to be effective, supervisees must participate and engage with the process. In group supervision, every group member should have an opportunity to bring something to the session. It is the supervisors' job to facilitate the sessions; however, each member of the group has a responsibility to monitor their own involvement too, ensuring they do not speak over other people or take up too much time.

- *Feedback and evaluation:* The importance of feedback and evaluation is explained in Chapter 11. This should form part of the contract and staff should be made aware how often, and in what format, they will take place.

- *Note taking:* It is common practice for supervisors to take notes during sessions. The supervisor can use them as a reminder of what was discussed, and follow up where necessary, to ensure safeguarding discussions are recorded. It is important to let staff know that notes will be recorded and that they will be stored securely. Supervisees can also take notes if they wish.

Boundaries

In schools, it is important to remind staff what supervision is and why they are there. Explain, again, the differences between counselling and supervision. It is important that staff understand that supervision is a space to explore work matters but, on occasion, personal issues may be impacting their work and how they are managing these (or vice versa). They may find it useful to talk about this in supervision, but they must feel safe to do so. In group supervision, it is vital to keep in mind that all members of the group are work colleagues and may feel vulnerable or regret sharing after the session. A discussion about this when setting the contract is beneficial.

An internal supervisor would need to discuss the boundaries regarding their role as supervisor and any other roles they have in school. It is important that everyone is clear about this and sticks to the boundaries discussed and agreed.

Confidentiality

A supervision contract must cover confidentiality and its limits in supervision; it could create problems if the supervisor is not clear with this. Although supervision is confidential, there are some situations where it would not be safe or ethical for the supervisor to keep the information to themselves:

- *Safeguarding:* If a safeguarding concern was brought to supervision that had not already been discussed with the DSL or headteacher, it would need to be shared outside of the supervisory relationship. This includes safeguarding concerns regarding a child, parent or member of staff.

- *Professional misconduct:* If the supervisor felt that a member of staff (either the supervisee or someone spoken about in supervision) had behaved in a manner that amounted to professional misconduct, it would need to be passed on to the headteacher.

It is impossible to anticipate every situation that may arise, but it is important that staff attending supervision understand that the supervisor has a duty of care to pass the information on, although it would be discussed with them first.

Supervisee confidentiality

In group supervision, the supervisees also have confidentiality to uphold on their part too. Every group member must agree to treat each other with professional respect and not discuss anything in supervision, with anyone else outside of the group. What is said in the group stays in the group.

If supervision is held online, then supervisees have a responsibility to find somewhere confidential to attend the session, ensuring no one else can overhear or interrupt. While it may be appropriate to sit in a coffee shop to attend some meetings, supervision is not one of them!

Session structure

During the first session, it is important to discuss what the sessions will look like. Each supervisee and every group will be different, so there is no set timetable for each session, but it is useful for those attending supervision to have an awareness of its structure:

- *Check-in and check-out:* Each session should begin with a brief check-in and end with a quick check-out; this could be a one-word answer, a number on a scale of 1–10 or a more detailed overview. The check-in ensures the supervisor (and the rest of the group in group supervision) has an understanding of how the supervisee is at the start of the session. Some may find this strange or uncomfortable to start with and not know what to say. Others may use it as an opportunity to offload. The check-in helps the supervisor to assess how the supervisee is feeling before the session begins.

  The check-out at the end of the session encourages the supervisee to reflect on the session, what was discussed and how they are feeling. The check-out also helps the supervisor to evaluate how the session has been for the supervisee.

  The check-ins/outs are an important part of supervision as they clearly define the start and end of each session, creating a boundary around it: 'Good beginnings set the shape of the session and good endings assist the learning to be contained, valued and transported into good practice' (Davys and Beddoe 2010, p.93).

- *Expectations:* The expectations of the supervisor and supervisees need to be discussed during the first session.

At this point, it is helpful to briefly explain the role of the supervisor and offer those in attendance the opportunity to ask any questions. It is also important to reassure supervisees that any notes the supervisor takes are for their own use, and that they will be locked away securely.

As a supervisor, I ask all supervisees to prepare for future sessions by thinking about what they would like to bring beforehand. I suggest that they make a note of anything that arises between sessions, so they do not forget them. I also recommend supervisees bring a notebook and pen so they can jot down anything of importance during sessions.

Setting a session agenda

It is important to remember that supervision is a reflective space for staff, so the agenda should be set by their needs. The supervisor may need to support the supervisee to pinpoint the most pressing issue/s to bring, but ultimately, the supervisor wants the supervisee to identify a problem and resolve it themselves.

For supervisees to gain the most benefit from supervision, it is important that time is spent setting the agenda at the start of each session. In order not to get bogged down with discussing organizational issues (as can happen with internal supervision), the supervisor needs to be skilled in helping the supervisee to stay focused on the aim of the session; the narrative should not take over so there is no time for reflection.

The following are the only 'set' agenda items for each session.

At the beginning

- Check-in.

- The supervisee shares what they would like to bring to

the session. In group supervision, I ask each person to present one thing they would like to discuss.

Nearing the end

- An evaluation of the session – 'How has the session been for you?'

- Check-out.

The time in between is spent on what the supervisee brings. At this point, it is useful for the supervisor to keep in mind Kolb's experiential learning cycle (introduced in Chapter 1) so they can support the supervisee to reflect, explore and learn from the situation. The supervisor can encourage this by listening, questioning (using mostly open questions) and giving feedback.

Useful questions for the supervisor to ask in supervision
Experience

- What have you brought to supervision today?

- What happened?

- What would you have liked to happen?

- What was happening before the incident?

- What was the trigger?

- How did you react (physically)?

- How did you respond (verbally)?

- How did other staff respond?

- How did you record the incident?

Reflection

- How did you feel at the time?

- How do you feel now?

- When have you felt like this before?

- How do you feel about the pupil?

- Do they remind you of another pupil/person?

- Does this situation remind you of an experience before?

- What stopped you from...?

- How does the situation affect you?

- What might be going on for the pupil/parent/colleague?

- What assumptions did you make?

- When you think about the behaviour, how does it make you feel?

- When have you felt like that before?

- What is your biggest concern?

- Have you resolved an issue like this before?

- What did you do?

Thinking

- What were you thinking at the time?

- What do you think now?

- What did you learn about yourself?

- What did you learn about the pupil/parent/colleague?

- What might help you make sense of the situation?

- What does the school expect of you?

- What are your strengths?

- What areas do you need to work on?

- What could you do/have done differently?

- What are the current risks?

- What are the limitations?

- For the issue to be resolved, what needs to happen?

- Do you have a clear understanding of the procedures in place to help you manage this (e.g., safeguarding/behaviour/whistleblowing)?

- Have you considered...?

Doing

- What are you responsible for in this situation?

- What are you going to do first?

- How are you going to approach it?

- What possible response/outcome are you concerned about, and how can we mitigate it?

- What would you like to happen?

- Who do you need support from?

- Do you need support from me (the supervisor)?

- How will you keep a record of this?

- What would be a successful outcome?

Psychological theories

School supervisors are not expected to be psychologists or counsellors, but it would be useful for them to have some understanding of key psychological theories. I recommend the following:

- Carl Rogers' core conditions (1957)

- John Bowlby's attachment theory (1969)

- The trauma cycle

- ACEs (Adverse Childhood Experiences) and toxic stress

- TA (transactional analysis) (Berne 1964)

- CBT (cognitive behavioural therapy): thought, feeling, behaviour cycle

- Mindfulness/relaxation strategies.

And finally...

If you are concerned about a member of staff's mental health, it is important that you support and direct them to further support:

- In an emergency, call 999.

- Book a GP appointment to discuss concerns. They can refer/signpost and offer medication where necessary.

- Samaritans provide emotional support to anyone in emotional distress, struggling to cope or at risk of suicide (www.samaritans.org, Tel: 116 123).

- Education Support is a charity dedicated to supporting the mental health and wellbeing of teachers and education staff in schools, colleges and universities (www.educationsupport.org.uk).

- Mental Health Matters is a nationwide charity providing a wide range of support to people with mental health needs (www.mhm.org.uk).

- PAPYRUS UK (under-35s) is a UK charity dedicated to the prevention of suicide and the promotion of positive mental health and emotional wellbeing in young people (www.papyrus-uk.org).

- Mind provides advice and support to empower anyone experiencing a mental health problem (www.mind. org.uk).

- SANE is a UK charity providing emotional support and information to anyone affected by mental illness (www. sane.org.uk).

- Text 'Shout' is a free, confidential, anonymous text support service. You can text 85258 from wherever you are in the UK (https://giveusashout.org).

Chapter 10 reflections and planning

✳ What would you like to add/change to your school supervision contract?

✳ What are your thoughts about the session agenda?

CHAPTER 11

Staff Feedback and Evaluation

The development of the supervision practice in schools should be a continuous process that values staff feedback and suggestions. The information can then be used to alter practice (where necessary), influence policy and develop further training for staff and the supervisor.

The importance of staff input

It can be all too easy for senior leaders to assume they know what staff want, or need, but it is important to remember that only the staff can know for sure. For example, when trying to improve staff mental health and wellbeing, we could assume a reduction in workload is the answer (and sometimes that may be the case); however, if staff feel valued and supported in their job role, they will be better equipped to manage the responsibilities they have. Often, initiatives that are put in place to support staff mental health and wellbeing are quick-fixes rather than long-term, systemic changes to the culture of the school; we need to be proactive rather than reactive when thinking about staff wellbeing.

An issue that comes up time and time again in schools is communication. When leaders are making big changes in school that directly involve staff (such as supervision), it is vital that they are included in the decision making; it should not be *done for them*, but rather, something they are *part of*.

Before finalizing your plans for supervision and writing your policy I suggest that the leadership team creates a staff survey asking them what *they* need to feel supported in their role. The responses will highlight what the needs are and how staff are really feeling. I suggest the survey is anonymous, so staff are able to respond honestly.

In the early stages of planning supervision in my own school, the feedback from staff provided invaluable information about what they felt was needed. Here are some of their thoughts:

Opportunities to share and discuss stresses shared with other teachers.

Dedicated time to discuss own concerns.

More support with children's mental health as this can affect ours.

Time away from school day factored in to allow reflection.

To be able to open up without the fear of judgement.

Greater recognition of good work.

To feel like I am able to communicate my feelings regarding work.

Encouraging me when I do things right, showing me that I'm a valued member of staff.

Having time to discuss our feelings and problems within the work environment.

Quiet spaces for adults as well as children.

Possibly having a session each term to touch base and talk to someone privately without trying to rush a conversation into what time you can find.

Time to talk with fellow colleagues.

Termly meetings, possibly with a peer, to discuss wellbeing.

I keep things to myself until it gets too much to deal with. I need to speak to others sooner.

That we learn to take notice of how others are feeling and give them that support.

Times to reflect.

Dedicated time for staff wellbeing.

Initiatives that promote a positive outlook on mental health in the workplace.

Dedicated time for staff to talk about concerns.

Time for reflection away from the school day.

Maybe a safe space for adults.

Time to support each other.

Having an environment where people are encouraged to discuss their wellbeing, and anything that can be changed to improve it.

Support groups.

These opinions and suggestions from staff helped our school to develop a model of supervision that would achieve many outcomes they desired, as well as the objectives identified by the school leaders.

Staff feedback

Feedback from staff continues to be just as valuable when supervision is in place as it ensures that their collective voice is still being heard.

In my own school, we decided to do two reviews each academic year: one mid-year and one end-of-year, in the form of an anonymous online survey. As with the pre-supervision survey results, we have been able to use the feedback from these to ensure supervision is meeting the needs of the school, staff and pupils. Where suggestions are made, we try (within reason) to accommodate them.

To ensure supervision is effective and achieving its functions, it is useful to place staff feedback under the headings of 'Formative/educative', 'Restorative/supportive' and 'Normative/managerial'.

Formative/educative

It's changed the way I have felt/dealt with personal and professional situations and made me realize that others feel the same.

It's a really good forum for discussion and helps to converse with other staff about successes/issues.

I have found the opportunity to share ideas, problems and possible solutions helpful.

I value the opportunity each term to have a professional discussion with colleagues from across the school.

Discussing issues with colleagues allows for a breadth of knowledge to be shared.

Listening to others' experiences and how they have dealt with certain situations.

I feel more reflective in my practice, and advice given during and after the session is taken on board.

It has made me re-evaluate the way I am seen at work and a way of being heard. It has also been useful to think about the way I work and interact with people.

The resource of other people's experience and viewpoints is really helpful in dealing with difficult issues in the classroom and it gives you time to reflect on your own practice.

Discussing particular trials and tribulations of the classroom (and also listening to other people's) makes me see the bigger picture and helps me think things through in a way that I may not have otherwise done.

You may pick up ideas from colleagues on how to handle a situation. I have sounded out ideas in supervision, which has been really useful.

It's useful to hear other professional voices to support in areas that you would like advice in.

Sharing ideas and strategies and implementing these.

Restorative/supportive

Having a designated platform to discuss current issues and the feeling of being listened to.

Just taking the time to talk has relieved the pressure that builds up naturally. It has been cathartic to have those very human conversations in a constructive and effective way.

On a personal level being able to discuss work stresses has meant I have been able to leave my 'work worries' at work.

Safe environment. Ability to be honest and share thoughts and opinions.

It has helped to network with other colleagues and to see that others may be feeling/experiencing similar to you. It has also helped to develop skills of reflection and allowed time to reflect, which can be hard to come by! I also think being given time like this to discuss things is a good start in recognizing the importance of teacher wellbeing in what is a demanding role.

As somebody who does not typically share my feelings about things too easily, I find it incredibly cathartic to have an open and safe discussion. I always leave feeling like a weight has been lifted.

Safe and open space to share feelings and discuss things without a fear of being judged.

People were very supportive and open and not at all judgemental. The sessions were well led, and I was 100 per cent confident that issues discussed always remained confidential.

Supervision has enabled me to voice and share concerns in a supportive and constructive environment.

You can discuss ideas in a confidential setting among other professionals – I find this really helpful.

Normative/managerial

It allows a chance to meet as a set of professionals and discuss key issues.

I have found that the time and space to articulate my thoughts aloud to myself and others have helped to clarify my thinking, put my concerns into some perspective, take ideas from others and identify areas that can be acted on.

I think it's made me feel more confident in voicing my concerns and feelings generally, so I am more competent in my role.

Strategies suggested have helped me to move forward with specific children.

Through discussions in supervision, it has given me ideas to take back to the class or to my teaching practice.

It's well structured, with time to reflect, share ideas and thoughts and to think forward.

The feedback received from our staff over the last three years has ensured that the functions of supervision are being achieved, as well as the needs identified by staff before supervision began.

Staff suggestions

All suggestions made by staff, no matter how small, are useful. Feedback from staff should help to shape the way supervision is run and ensure that they feel their input is listened to and actioned where possible. The suggestions here are good examples of this:

Maybe each person could have time at the beginning (just after or during check-ins) to briefly tell you things that they may have had in mind – prior to supervision – to talk about. This way, we can look at overlaps and merge them. It will also mean that other discussions won't go on for too long in order to ensure there is enough time to discuss other things highlighted at the beginning of each session.

Sometimes I found that I raise issues at the end of the session because I don't feel it's appropriate to raise it during the check-in, and then it doesn't feel appropriate when we are discussing other points. Not sure if this is the case with others too. Should I be bringing these up during the check-in?

I would prefer to be in a more spaced-out environment. Perhaps the table could be turned a different way during supervision to facilitate this.

Some feedback cannot bring about change quickly due to the logistics that are involved. Later down the line, they may be possible:

I do find it hard to go straight into my role afterwards. It would be nice to have 10 minutes to reflect after before jumping straight into the classroom.

While there may be times that operational changes cannot be made, it is still useful for schools to have an awareness of potential barriers for staff:

Unfortunately, sessions were on my day off. My intent was to still take part because I think it is a useful opportunity to share, discuss, listen, etc., but sadly it did not fit in with my schedule.

Evaluation of impact and effectiveness

Supervision reviews will help schools to evaluate if supervision is meeting the needs of staff and the school. Reviewing supervision regularly also helps to measure its impact, effectiveness and quality.

Since introducing supervision at our school in 2019, the reviews that take place twice a year have helped inform our policies and procedures. The results over the last three years have shown that supervision has been useful to staff, and it has positively impacted their practice as professionals.

In response to the question 'Have you found supervision useful?', the findings were very positive (see Figures 11.1 and 11.2).

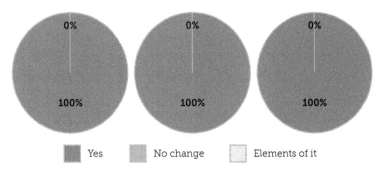

Figure 11.1: Teacher responses

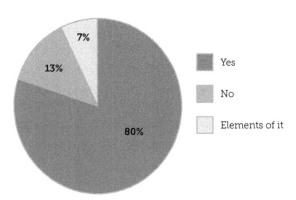

Figure 11.2: Support staff responses

In response to the question 'Has supervision had a positive impact on you professionally?', the findings were also positive (see Figure 11.3).

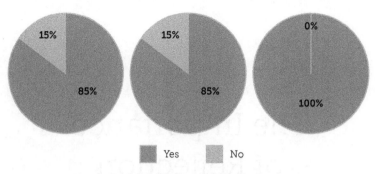

Figure 11.3: Teacher responses

Statements from staff at my own school highlight how valuable supervision can be to individuals and the whole school community:

They [supervision sessions] are incredibly valuable and are such an essential part of our school and for our wellbeing. It's great to have the time to share thoughts, feelings and offer advice in a confidential place and feel listened to.

I feel very positive about our whole-school team and the way we are led, and supervision plays a big part in this. I think I always knew that I am listened to and valued, but supervision has really enhanced this.

Chapter 11 reflections and planning

* Will staff be asked to complete a survey before supervision begins? If so, what questions will you ask?

* How will you review the effectiveness of supervision?

* How often will you review it?

CHAPTER 12

The Importance of Reflection

Reflective learning is at the core of reflective supervision in schools: 'supervision is a forum for learning and that the main vehicle for learning is reflection' (Davys and Beddoe 2009, p.920). Reflection is a skill that must be practised, however, and as a member of staff at my own school has identified, when do we have the time to stop and reflect when everyday life is so busy, in and out of school?

> *The ever-increasing pace of work, particularly when juggling a role outside of school as well, i.e., parent, has meant that I have been less reflective than I used to be because of lack of time. If only once a term now I do have 'permission' and time to reflect on experiences and feelings.*

As well as David Kolb, Donald Schön, philosopher and professor, has been pivotal in the development of reflective learning. Schön defined reflective practice as the practice by which professionals become aware of their implicit knowledge base and learn from their experience. He identified two central forms of reflection: reflection 'in action' and reflection 'on action' (1991).

Reflection in action refers to the decisions people make

during their everyday lives. According to Davys and Beddoe, this involves 'conscious considerations, evaluations and decision-making' (2010, p.92). Reflection on action is 'the consideration, analysis and evaluation' of the event after it has taken place (2010, p.92). Reflective supervision encourages staff to reflect on action – to think about their experiences, evaluate their responses and learn from them. The knowledge gained from this should, over time, increase their ability to reflect in action, that is, to 'think on their feet': 'When a supervisee internalises the processes of reflective learning these can be accessed as a tool for "in action" reflection' (2010, p.105).

The 'reflective cycle' was developed by sociologist and psychologist Graham Gibbs in 1988. This model built on Kolb's experiential learning cycle but added an element of critical reflection. As with action reflection, critical reflection enables you to make connections between your experiences, what you learned from them and how you will apply that knowledge in the future. Gibbs identified that 'it is not sufficient to have an experience in order to learn...without reflecting on the experience it may be quickly forgotten or its learning potential lost' (from Gibbs 1988, p.9).

Reflective supervision provides staff with the opportunity to practise their reflection skills, increasing their self-awareness so they are more able to make conscious, well thought-out decisions at work rather than reacting in the moment or responding in the same way over and over again. A teacher in my own school recognized the importance of this:

> *I feel that I am more child-centred in terms of their well-being and my concerns about the busyness of the school day. Through acknowledging and sharing my awareness of when I am feeling stressed to do with workload and, particularly, the pressures of a packed curriculum, I feel that I am making better decisions about how much to*

tackle on any one day. I believe that being more mindful of these pressures and making better decisions will help to maintain a healthy, happy classroom where children are not pressured to move from one task to another so quickly.

The DfE's *Teachers' Standards* (2011, p.7) stipulate: 'Appropriate self-evaluation, reflection and professional development activity is critical to improving teachers' practice at all career stages'; reflective supervision in education provides the perfect space for this to take place.

In feedback from my own school, staff recognized the positive impact reflective supervision has had on them:

It gave me time to reflect and I felt confident that I would have the support of others following discussions with my group.

I think it forces me to take the time to reflect on my own experiences and those of others, which, ordinarily, in a very busy working environment, can be very difficult.

It gives me time to reflect in a safe place where I know I won't be judged for what I say and how I feel.

I think it is important to have time to reflect on how you are feeling and why. An insight into other people's feelings and experiences can sometimes help unpick your own. It's good to relate to others in ways you may not be able to do daily as it can help put your own worries, doubts or feelings into perspective.

It has helped me be more of a reflective practitioner and look at things from a broader point of view.

*It's given me a chance to reflect on my growth through-
out the year.*

My own reflections of supervision in education

There is still a long way to go until supervision is embedded
within education. It is going to take time and dedication from
school leaders for it to become common practice. Introducing
something new and unknown can be scary and unsettling to
begin with, for leaders and staff. What I can tell you from my
own experience is that it will be worth it. It hasn't always gone
smoothly, though. Operational changes within school have
meant that I have had to restructure how I run supervision
a couple of times, and in the moment, it is disheartening and
frustrating, but I always manage to find a way around it. I
have no doubt that this will happen again at some point in the
future, but, like before, I will work around it.

This book is not going to provide all the answers for every
school – it would be impossible to do so – but I hope at the
very least that it will start conversations in schools. I hope that
education staff reading this will *at least start* thinking about
how reflective supervision could work in their own school. It
can be daunting to try something outside of the status quo, but
I suspect that if you are reading this book, it is because you feel
a change needs to take place in education; what you decide to
do with that feeling is down to you.

My wish is for *all* schools to have a whole-school approach
to mental health and wellbeing, and that supervision is part of
it so staff and pupils can be reflective, eager learners, in every
part of their lives:

We must trust our feelings and risk the challenges of new
experiences. Let's rededicate ourselves to provide learning
communities that kids love and that are rewarding for adults.

To accomplish that goal, we must step back and trust our students and ourselves and give us all the freedom to learn. (Rogers 1983, p.375)

References

Anna Freud National Centre for Children and Families (2020) *Supporting Staff Wellbeing in Schools.* Accessed on 15/12/2022 at www.annafreud. org/media/11451/3rdanna-freud-booklet-staff-wellbeing-new-address-april-2020.pdf

Atkinson, J. (1989) 'Responding to Elton: A whole school approach.' *Support for Learning 4*, 4, 242–248. Accessed on 23/01/2023 at https://nasenjournals. onlinelibrary.wiley.com/doi/10.1111/j.1467-9604.1989.tb00375.x

Barnardo's Scotland (2019) *Supporting the Mental Health and Wellbeing of Education Staff Through Professional Supervision Structures.* Trauma Informed Schools – Discussion Paper #1. June. Accessed on 15/12/2022 at www. barnardos.org.uk/sites/default/files/uploads/supporting-mental-health-wellbeing-education-staff-through-professional-supervision-structures. pdf

Berne, E. (1964) *Games People Play.* New York: Grove Press.

Billinghurst, G. (2021) 'Learning models, coaching and change management.' Cateran, 21 March. Accessed on 15/12/2022 at https://cateran.ie/ learning-models-coaching-and-change-management

Bowlby, J. (1969) *Attachment and Loss. Vol. 1, Attachment.* London: Penguin.

Carnegie School of Education (2020) 'NHSE Professional Learning Programmes 2020–2021.' Accessed on 15/12/2022 at https://issuu. com/carnegieschooleducation/docs/nhse_professional_learning_ programmes_2020-2021_is

Davys, A. M. and Beddoe, L. (2009) 'The reflective learning model: Supervision of social work students.' *Social Work Education 28*, 8, 919–933. Accessed on 15/12/2022 at www.utas.edu.au/__data/assets/pdf_file/0006/1237749/ Social-Work-Reflective-Learning-Model-Davys-and-Beddoe.pdf

Davys, A. M. and Beddoe, L. (2010) *Best Practice in Professional Supervision: A Guide for the Helping Professions.* London: Jessica Kingsley Publishers.

DfE (Department for Education) (2011) *Teachers' Standards: Guidance for School Leaders, School Staff and Governing Bodies.* July. Accessed on 15/12/2022 at https://assets.publishing.service.gov.uk/government/

uploads/system/uploads/attachment_data/file/1040274/Teachers__Standards_Dec_2021.pdf

DfE (2018) *Mental Health and Behaviour in Schools*. November. Accessed on 23/01/2023 at www.gov.uk/government/publications/mental-health-and-behaviour-in-schools--2

DfE (2021a) *The Education Staff Wellbeing Charter*. Accessed on 15/12/2022 at https://assets.publishing.service.gov.uk/government/uploads/system/uploads/attachment_data/file/1034032/DfE_Education_Workforce_Welbeing_Charter_Nov21.pdf

DfE (2021b) *Statutory Framework for the Early Years Foundation Stage: Setting the Standards for Learning, Development and Care for Children from Birth to Five*. Accessed on 15/12/2022 at https://assets.publishing.service.gov.uk/government/uploads/system/uploads/attachment_data/file/974907/EYFS_framework_-_March_2021.pdf

DfE (2022) *Keeping Children Safe in Education 2022: Statutory Guidance for Schools and Colleges*. Accessed on 15/12/2022 at https://assets.publishing.service.gov.uk/government/uploads/system/uploads/attachment_data/file/1101454/Keeping_children_safe_in_education_2022.pdf

Downing, N. (2019) 'Wellbeing: Why don't schools offer staff supervision?' *Tes Magazine*, 27 June. Accessed on 15/12/2022 at www.tes.com/magazine/archived/wellbeing-why-dont-schools-offer-staff-supervision

Education Support (2020) *Teacher Wellbeing Index 2020*. Accessed on 15/12/2022 at www.educationsupport.org.uk/media/yfrhfjca/teacher_wellbeing_index_2020.pdf

Education Support (2021) *Teacher Wellbeing Index 2021*. Accessed on 15/12/2022 at www.educationsupport.org.uk/media/qzna4gxb/twix-2021.pdf

Education Support (no date) School leaders' service | Wellbeing services | Help for your staff | Get help. Accessed on 15/12/2022 at www.educationsupport.org.uk/get-help/help-for-your-staff/wellbeing-services/school-leaders-service

Geddes, H. (2017) *Attachment in Classroom: A Practical Guide for Schools*. London: Worth Publishing.

Gibbs, G. (1988) *Learning by Doing: A Guide to Teaching and Learning Methods*. Oxford: Further Education Unit, Oxford Polytechnic.

Haig, M. (2021) *The Comfort Book*. Edinburgh: Canongate.

Hartley, P. and Kennard, D. (2009) *Staff Support Groups in the Helping Professions: Principles, Practice and Pitfalls*. Hove: Routledge.

Hawkins, P. and Shohet, R. (2012) *Supervision in the Helping Professions*. Maidenhead: Open University Press.

Inskipp, F. and Proctor, B. (1993) *Making the Most of Supervision: A Professional Development Resource for Counsellors, Supervisors and Trainees*. Twickenham: Cascade.

In-Trac Training and Consultancy Ltd (2022) 'Education...' Accessed on 15/12/2022 at www.in-trac.co.uk/schools

Kolb, D. A. (1984) *Experiential Learning: Experience as the Source of Learning and Development*. Englewood Cliffs, NJ: Prentice-Hall.

Lawrence, N. (2020a) *Supervision in Education – Healthier Schools for All. Barnardo's Scotland Report on the Use of Professional or Reflective Supervision in Education*. Trauma-informed Schools – Paper #2. Barnardo's Scotland. Accessed on 15/12/2020 at www.barnardos.org.uk/sites/default/files/uploads/Supervision%20in%20Education%20-%20Healthier%20Schools%20For%20All%20-%20Main%20report_1.pdf

Lawrence, N. (2020b) *Supervision in Education – Healthier Schools for All. Barnardo's Scotland Report on the Use of Professional or Reflective Supervision in Education*. Executive Summary. Barnardo's Scotland. Accessed on 15/12/2022 at www.barnardos.org.uk/sites/default/files/uploads/Supervision%20in%20Education%20-%20Healthier%20Schools%20For%20All%20-%20Executive%20Summary_0.pdf

Maslow, A. H. ([1943] 2013) *A Theory of Human Motivation*. Radford, VA: Wilder Publications. [Originally published in the *Psychological Review 50*, 4, 370–396, in 1943.]

NHS (2021) *Mental Health of Children and Young People in England, 2021, Wave 2*. Accessed on 15/12/2022 at https://digital.nhs.uk/data-and-information/publications/statistical/mental-health-of-children-and-young-people-in-england/2021-follow-up-to-the-2017-survey

NHS Manchester University (2022) *Adverse Childhood Experiences (ACEs) and Attachment*. Accessed on 15/12/2022 at https://mft.nhs.uk/rmch/services/camhs/young-people/adverse-childhood-experiences-aces-and-attachment

Ofsted (2019) *Teacher Well-Being at Work in Schools and Further Education Providers*. Accessed on 15/12/2022 at https://assets.publishing.service.gov.uk/government/uploads/system/uploads/attachment_data/file/936253/Teacher_well-being_report_110719F.pdf

Proctor, B. (2008) *Group Supervision: A Guide to Creative Practice* (2nd edn). London: SAGE Publications.

Proctor, B. (2010) 'Training for the Supervision Alliance.' In B. Proctor, *Routledge Handbook of Clinical Supervision: Fundamental International Themes* (Chapter 3). Abingdon: Routledge. Accessed on 25/09/2022 at www.routledgehandbooks.com/doi/10.4324/9780203843437.ch3

Reed, J. (2008) 'Freeing the Passion to Learn.' In R. Shohet (ed.) *Passionate Supervision* (Chapter 9). London: Jessica Kingsley Publishers.

Rioch, M. J., Coulter, W. R. and Weinberger, D. M. (1976) *Dialogues for Therapists*. San Francisco: Jossey-Bass.

Rogers, C. R. (1957) 'The necessary and sufficient conditions of therapeutic personality change.' *Journal of Consulting Psychology 21*, 2, 95–103. Accessed on 23/01/2023 at https://doi.org/10.1037/h0045357

Rogers, C. R. (1983) *Freedom to Learn for the 80's*. New York: Merrill.

Sayer, A. (2021) *Supporting Staff Mental Health in Your School.* London: Jessica Kingsley Publishers.

Schön, D. A. (1991) *The Reflective Practitioner: How Professionals Think in Action.* Aldershot: Ashgate.

Shakespeare, W. (2000) *Romeo and Juliet* (Wordsworth Classics). Ware: Wordsworth Editions.

Sturt, P. and Rowe, J. (2018) *Using Supervision in Schools: A Guide to Building Safe Cultures and Providing Emotional Support in a Range of School Settings.* Hove: Pavilion.

Tuckman, B. W. (1965) 'Developmental sequence in small groups.' *Psychological Bulletin 63*, 384–399. Accessed on 15/12/2022 at https://pubmed.ncbi.nlm.nih.gov/14314073

Weston, L. L. (2022) 'Teacher wellbeing is the beginning of pupil wellbeing.' Dreamachine blog, 21 September. Accessed on 15/12/2022 at https://dreamachine.world/2022/09/21/teacher-well-being-blog

Yalom, I. (1985) *The Theory and Practice of Group Psychotherapy.* New York: Basic Books.

Further Reading

Bethune, A. (2018) *Wellbeing in the Primary Classroom: A Practical Guide to Teaching Happiness and Positive Mental Health.* London: Bloomsbury Publishing.

Bethune, A. and Kell, E. (2020) *A Little Guide for Teachers: Teacher Wellbeing and Self-Care.* London: SAGE Publishing.

Bomber, L. (2007) *Inside I'm Hurting: Practical Strategies for Supporting Children with Attachment Difficulties in Schools.* London: Worth Publishing.

Brooks, R. (2019) *The Trauma and Attachment-Aware Classroom: A Practical Guide to Supporting Children Who Have Encountered Trauma and Adverse Childhood Experiences.* London: Jessica Kingsley Publishers.

Knightsmith, P. (2019) *The Mentally Healthy Schools Workbook: Practical Tips, Ideas, Action Plans and Worksheets for Making Meaningful Change.* London: Jessica Kingsley Publishers.

Meek, L., Jordan, S. and McKinley, S. (2020) *Mental Health and Wellbeing in Secondary Education: A Practical Guide and Resource.* Hove: Pavilion.

Rae, T. (2020) *A Toolbox of Wellbeing: Helpful Strategies and Activities for Children, Teens, Their Carers and Teachers.* Banbury: Hinton House Publishers.

Video Clips

Charlie Waller Trust (no date) 'Top tips for setting up staff supervision groups in schools.' Accessed on 20/04/2023 at https://charliewaller.org/resources/supervision-in-education

Talking Heads (16 November 2018) 'Supervision curious – Why supervision in education is essential.' Accessed on 15/12/2022 at www.youtube.com/watch?v=DkSR5PUi26M

Trauma Informed Schools UK (no date) 'Reflective supervision in schools.' Accessed on 15/12/2022 at www.traumainformedschools.co.uk/online-supervision/free-supervision-webinar

Index

Supporting Staff Mental Health in Your School

Amy Sayer
Foreword by Pooky Knightsmith

£14.99 | $21.95 | PB | 160PP |

ISBN 978 1 78775 463 8 |

eISBN 978 1 78775 464 5

This is an accessible guide for schools explaining how to implement effective techniques to improve staff mental health. Drawing on case studies from years of experience supporting staff mental health, Amy Sayer introduces inexpensive, practical and realistic strategies that schools can implement to ensure the mental wellbeing of teaching staff.

This book provides steps to ensure that self-care and family time do not slip under the radar in the face of increasing pressure and limited resources. From providing adequate staffroom facilities to ensuring that teachers can set clear boundaries around weekends and break times, these ideas create and foster a culture of openness around mental health and help teachers to re-discover their love of teaching.

Amy Sayer is a teacher at Chichester High School and Head of Philosophy and Ethics. She has previously been MH Lead and responsible for supporting disadvantaged children. She has written articles for *Teach Secondary*, *SecEd* and *TES*.

The Mentally Healthy Schools Workbook

Practical Tips, Ideas, Action Plans and Worksheets for Making Meaningful Change

Pooky Knightsmith
Foreword by Norman Lamb

£19.99 | $27.95 | PB | 200PP |
ISBN 978 1 78775 148 4 |
eISBN 978 1 78775 149 1

This book is the perfect starting point for anyone looking to promote and encourage mental health in their school. It covers not only the day-to-day practical steps you can take to meet the mental health needs of learners, but also provides a whole bank of ideas for making meaningful change in your school.

Pooky Knightsmith draws on the latest thinking and policy on mental health to expertly lay out tried and tested tools you can use to evaluate the overall mental health of your school. She shows how to improve and support the mental health of staff, and how to make sure that the voice of every learner is heard and valued, including the most vulnerable – and how to ensure that everyone involved with the school feels safe, healthy and happy.

Pooky Knightsmith has a PhD in child mental health from the Institute of Psychiatry, is the author of five books and is the current chair of the Children and Young People's Mental Health Coalition. She has a YouTube channel which is a source of Continuing Professional Development for many educators in the UK and beyond.

The Mental Health and Wellbeing Handbook for Schools

Transforming Mental Health Support on a Budget

Clare Erasmus
Foreword by Chris Edwards

£18.99 | $26.95 | PB | 144PP |

ISBN 978 1 78592 481 1 |

eISBN 978 1 78450 869 2

This book lays out an intuitive and practical approach to mental health and wellbeing that any school can adopt to transform their mental health support for students.

With a focus on providing staff on a limited budget with practical tools, the book helps schools make a real difference to student mental health. It sets out a roadmap for staff to create robust mental health support for students without requiring qualifications in psychology or counselling. It covers key areas including staff training, creating safe spaces for wellbeing and how to harness the support of parents and the local community. It also includes practical advice for addressing concerns such as stress, self-harm and body image. From small, everyday improvements that foster a culture of mental wellbeing to whole school campaigns, this book shows how to embed mental health at the heart of a school's philosophy.

Clare Erasmus has 20 years' teaching experience and is head of whole school mental health and wellbeing at Brighton Hill Community School and creator of the TedX talk #familyMH5aday. She currently lives in Portsmouth, UK.